The
Gay Agenda
2016

All Fronts

Juan Ahonen-Jover, Ph.D.

Book website: www.GayAgenda2016.com

Cover based on photo by Jason Doiy

Dedication

This book is for all persons who
believe in the equality expressed in the
United States Declaration of Independence—

**"We hold these truths to be self-evident, that all men are
created equal"—**

and in the United States Constitution:

**"Nor deny to any person within its jurisdiction the equal
protection of the laws."**

Books in This Series

The Gay Agenda is the most comprehensive guidebook for achieving legal equality for lesbian, gay, bisexual, and transgender Americans (LGBT). The only book like it, it gets updated yearly with specific action plans for that year.

The Gay Agenda 2012: All Out

The Gay Agenda 2013: All In

The Gay Agenda 2014: Don't Stop

The Gay Agenda 2015: Loving & More

The Gay Agenda 2016: All Fronts

What Readers Are Saying

"I love this book."
   —Jennifer Molho
     Amazon Reviewer

"This is a wonderful book! The way it is written makes it good for LGBT people and beyond. The layout makes it easy to read."
   —L.G. Gracey
     President, Grace Concepts

"This is an excellent read, an incredibly important contribution to the LGBT community, and an important work. Thanks for keeping it up to date."
   —Stephen E. Herbits
     Activist donor

"With true stories and personal tidbits, Dr. Jover weaves a powerful narrative from start to finish detailing why it is high time that we unite and work to ensure true legal equality for our LGBT brothers and sisters."
   —Sailesh K. Rao
     Executive Director, Climate Healers

"This is an easily read book from the inside of the LGBT activist community. Juan knows about what he writes."
   —David L. Andreas
     Retired Bank Executive

Is This Book for *You?*

This book is for believers only. Do you firmly believe in the principle of treating everybody equally under the law?

- If you are seeking to understand the most important social issue of our generation, this book is for you (especially Part I and the epilogue).

- If you are a parent or grandparent interested in family values and protecting your children, this book is for you (especially Parts I, II, and the epilogue).

- If you are a policy maker of any party affiliation who wants to write laws that are fair, this book is for you (read it all).

- If you are a religious person interested in preserving your freedom of religion, this book is for you (especially Part I and the epilogue).

- If your sexual orientation or gender identity or expression does not fit that of the majority, this book is for you. You may know some of the information presented, but you will gain more insights and inspiration for fighting for equal treatment under the law (read especially Part IV and the epilogue and *take action*).

- If you are a believer in equality, this book is for you. You may know some of the book's content, but read especially Part IV and the epilogue all and *take action*.

- If you have read any of the prior editions of *The Gay Agenda*, read Part IV in detail since it describes the actions to take in 2016.

Contents

Preface

We the people are under attack. From freedom of religion and family values, to individualism and the pursuit of happiness, our core beliefs are constantly being challenged. Indeed, we have recently won some monumental battles, but, nonetheless, we must remain steadfast in our efforts to protect the principles set forth in our Constitution and achieve the full equality it guarantees us.

The *Gay Agenda* book series is a comprehensive collection of guidebooks for achieving LGBT (lesbian, gay, bisexual, transgender) equality under US law. Updated annually, it takes a look at current trends, accomplishments, and setbacks in the gay agenda and describes ways you can act to further fuel the movement. It is the most comprehensive guidebook available for achieving LGBT equality and makes a timely call for action

This 2016 edition, recounts familiar fundamentals such as what the gay agenda is, the impetuses for action, and other long-term LGBT goals and adds new considerations to the ongoing conversation within and around the LGBT community. Included are a list of ten actions you can take this year; strategic and creative donor methods; and, among many other things, ways to reach the president, legislature, and judicial system, as well as make your voice heard in the "other thirty states" that still remain blind to justice.

Part I describes what LGBT means and the arguments used to deny equal treatment under the law to this group of people.

Part II shows what the gay agenda is in detail, including the goals to be achieved.

Part III describes the different paths available to achieve equality.

Part IV details specific actions you can take in 2016 to reach legal equality for the LGBT community.

Finally, the epilogue describes the ultimate goal—beyond legal equality.

What We Accomplished in 2015

Here are the main advances in 2015:

- The US Supreme Court ruled that the US Constitution requires that all states and territories make the fundamental right of marriage available to all couples, independently of their sexual orientation. *This is the biggest victory for LGBT equality ever.*

  Gallup estimated that by the end of 2015 there were about one million Americans in same-sex marriages.

- The Equal Employment Opportunity Commission (EEOC) ruled that discrimination in employment due to sexual orientation is a form of sex discrimination. In 2012, the EEOC had a similar ruling regarding gender identity. By the charter of this commission, these rulings only apply to employment and not to housing, public accommodations, or credit.

- In several states, succeeded in stopping "freedom of religion" legislation that was intended to deny services and discriminate against LGBT people, as well as several "bathroom" laws that required transgender people to use the bathroom matching their gender at birth. Unfortunately, we did not win all these battles yet.

- The congressional LGBT Equality Caucus created a Task Force on Transgender Equality addressing the legislative needs for the community including health care, violence, unemployment, and homelessness. It is composed of eight members of congress (including Ileana Ros-Lehtinen (R-FL) who has a transgender son and Mike Honda (D-CA) who has a transgender granddaughter).

- Salt Lake City elected Jackie Biskupski, an openly lesbian, as its mayor.

- Pennsylvania confirmed Dr. Rachel Levine, a transgender woman, as its Physician General.

- The Boys Scouts of America rescinded the ban on gay adults being leaders of the organization. In 2013 the organization had removed the ban on gay youth being a member.

- Several courts ruled in favor on multiple cases challenging LBGT equality.

To review the annual accomplishments from 2012 to 2015 (the five years the *Gay Agenda* has been published, check Appendix 5.

Part I:

Who Are These LGBT People?

1.

Who Are These Lesbian, Gay, Bisexual, and Transgender (LGBT) People?

"I'm proud to be gay, and I consider being gay among the greatest gifts God has given me."

—Tim Cook, Apple CEO, October 30, 2014

They are your neighbors, your coworkers, your elected officials (even if you may not realize it), your children or grandchildren (even if they do not know it yet). They are a small part of the population, but they are everywhere—in every culture, religion, location, and profession. Some live as couples, some as singles, and some are married to somebody of the opposite gender. What they all have in common is that their sexual orientation or gender identity or how they express their gender is different from the majority.

Some are exclusively attracted to members of the same gender. Others are attracted to both genders. Others feel that their anatomical gender of birth does not correspond to the gender their minds tell them they belong to. We call these people *LGBT* as the abbreviation for *lesbian, gay, bisexual, and transgender.*

Other people prefer to call themselves *queer*, which is an all-encompassing term for anybody who does not want to be classified as heterosexual or gay or lesbian or bisexual or transgender. So, sometimes the term LGBTQ is also used to include *queer*. Also, the *Q* in LGBTQ can also mean questioning, to represent people who are questioning their sexuality.

There are also people who are intersex, meaning that, from birth, they have both male and female genital characteristics. So another term in use is LGBTQIA for *lesbian, gay, bisexual, transexual, queer or questioning, intersex, and ally.*

The term *two spirit* is used by some Native Americans to indicate gender variant individuals. Several books have been written on the topic.

There are also *asexual* people, who do not feel sexual attraction to others and are part of the spectrum of sexual orientation (check asexuality.org).

Here is another, more recent term*: metrosexual.* It describes mostly men who are hip, cool, and fashionable. They are very comfortable with people of a different sexual orientation and gender identity. Metrosexuals themselves can be of any sexual orientation or gender identity or expression, although most are heterosexual.

By now, you may think that this book is *not* for you, since you may be more interested in issues such as:

- Why can't everybody just get along, marry somebody of the opposite sex, have children, and be productive members of society?

- What type of a country are we building in the United States if we allow the collapse of the traditional family?

- What will happen if we abandon our bedrock principles of individuality, respect for religion, separation of religion from state, and separation of powers in the three government branches?

This book answers these important questions. To have an opinion is easy; to learn the facts and be open to modifying our opinions based on new information is harder. Hopefully, you are willing to read here about other points of view that, you may be surprised to discover, are closer to your opinions than you may think.

Let's start with some fundamentals.

The gay agenda is not only about lesbian, gay, bisexual, and transgender people (LGBT). It is about *every person* because each of us has a sexual orientation and a gender identity and expression. As uncomfortable as the topic may be to some people, it is a very important component of who we are as people. Notice that sexual orientation refers to heterosexuality, homosexuality, and bisexuality. So laws and rules that apply to sexual orientation protect *every* person, *including heterosexuals.*

The American Psychological Association defines sexual orientation as follows:
(www.apa.org/helpcenter/sexual-orientation.aspx)

> Sexual orientation refers to an enduring pattern of emotional, romantic, and/or sexual attractions to men, women, or both sexes. Sexual orientation also refers to a person's sense of identity based on those attractions, related behaviors, and membership in a community of others who share those attractions.

Besides sexual orientation, we need to understand gender identity and expression, which is defined by the American Psychological Association as follows:
(www.apa.org/topics/sexuality/transgender.aspx)

> Gender identity refers to a person's internal sense of being male, female, or something else; gender expression refers to the way a person communicates gender identity to others through behavior, clothing, hairstyles, voice, or body characteristics.

Like sexual orientation, gender identity affects every person. Most people feel comfortable that their gender at birth matches the gender that they feel they belong to; but some people feel differently. Some like to cross-dress, which is independent of sexual orientation (most cross-dressers are heterosexual—many in happy marriages). Others feel that they need to change their gender to the one they feel is their true gender.

Note that sexual orientation (the people to whom you are attracted) is different from gender identity (the gender to which you belong in your mind) and different from the expression of that gender. For instance, a male may have surgery to become a female (her gender identity is female) but at the same time be attracted to males (so her sexual orientation is heterosexual). In another example, a heterosexual female may like to dress manlier, so her gender expression may be that of a man despite that she is a heterosexual female. All the potential combinations can be mind-boggling the first time you hear about them, but life is complex and not just black and white.

For whatever reasons, some people cannot comprehend why transgender people need to change the gender of birth. However, America has a proud tradition of commitment to freedom, happiness, and individuality, so respect for others' freedom, especially about private personal matters, will eventually prevail.

Before we continue with the rest of the book, it is very important to understand that people who are gay or lesbian or bisexual or transgender are not weirdos; actually, many of them have made very important contributions to society (see a list in Appendix 1).

The next chapter talks about everyday life.

2.

A Day in the Life of a Family

The alarm goes off. It is 6:00 a.m. It seems that the alarm always goes off too early.

Lisa drags herself out of bed. She barely makes it to the kitchen, where the coffee is already brewing. Ah! What technology can do! You set it up the night before, and coffee is ready when you wake up.

Thanks to the coffee, Lisa makes it to the shower then wakes up the kids and prepares breakfast.

Mornings are always such a struggle. It is never easy with four children: Michael, Danielle, David, and Katie. Rush, rush, and rush. Lisa takes the kids to the school bus. Today is going to be a tough day. Katie, the youngest of the couple's children, is home with the flu.

The couple adopted their four children. Nobody wanted these children because they all have special needs: Drug exposure during pregnancy or HIV exposure in the womb or development delays. They are great kids, but, through no fault of their own, they were rejected by other adoptive parents. Fortunately, the two kids who were exposed to HIV in the womb have tested negative. Things are going well.

The rest of the morning flies by with going to the supermarket, taking care of Katie, and doing three loads of laundry.

In the afternoon, Lisa takes the kids to after-school activities. Lisa is a very busy stay-at-home mom. In addition, she teaches the first communion classes in her church. She is also the volunteer coordinator for her children's elementary school. And she also started two Girl Scout troops!

She is the supermom that even teenagers are proud of.

Lisa rushes home to prepare dinner. Just after 7:00 p.m., Janice, her partner of eighteen years, gets home. She is exhausted after a full day of work as a manager of a state child welfare program. She is well respected for her work and knowledge (with a master's in public administration and a master's in social work).

The conversation at the dinner table centers on the children. It always does. Lisa and Janice ask them how their day at school was, review their homework, and so on—the usual stuff.

By midnight, they both have fallen asleep on the couch, pretending to watch TV.

They feel blessed for what they have. Tomorrow surely the alarm will go off again at 6:00 a.m.

For these two moms, life is not different from that of any other couple with children.

Or so they thought.

3.

A Bad Day in the Life of a Family

Lisa and Janice—along with their three youngest children, Danielle, David, and Katie—flew from rainy western Washington to sunny Florida to board a family cruise to the Bahamas to celebrate the couple's anniversary.

This was a trip that the children (and their parents) had so much looked forward to. They were in line early to board the ship. They had lunch together just after 1:00 p.m. Everyone was excited about relaxing together as a family for an entire week. What a great adventure awaited them!

After lunch, the children asked impatiently to explore the ship and headed to the top deck, where they found a basketball court. A court on a cruise ship—what could be cooler?

Janice said she was going to unpack and take a siesta (nothing like taking on a Latin tradition while in Miami). The ship wasn't scheduled to depart until 3:00 p.m., so there was plenty of time before the sail-away party.

Lisa, never one to sit still, joined the children on the top deck with her coffee in one hand and a camera in the other, not different from what any mother would do. It was such a happy day.

While taking pictures of the children, Lisa suddenly collapsed on the basketball court, spilling her coffee and dropping the camera. The children, just nine years to twelve years old, helped pick up their mom and navigated their way down ten decks to find their cabin to bang on the door and wake up their other mom, Janice.

With the help of Janice, they flagged down a porter to get a wheelchair since Lisa was unable to stand on her own. The family headed immediately to the medical center onboard. The doctor established that Lisa was gravely ill. He then requested the ship's captain to delay departure and ordered an urgent transfer to the trauma center in Miami at Jackson Memorial Hospital. Medics arrived to take over emergency care of Lisa while a sheriff's deputy escorted Janice, the children, and their luggage to a waiting taxi. The taxi and medics carrying Lisa arrived at Ryder Trauma Center almost simultaneously around three-thirty in the afternoon.

Janice attempted to follow the gurney carrying Lisa through the emergency entrance but was asked to go to the waiting room and speak with the clerk. Janice settled the children in some chairs and headed to the desk to speak with the clerk. She asked to fill out admitting papers for Lisa, her partner, but was told to "take a seat" and wait for someone to come speak with her.

Some time later, a man appeared and introduced himself as Garnett Frederick, a hospital social worker. He then informed Janice that she and her family were in an "antigay city and state," and that if Janice wanted to find out about Lisa's condition or even see her, she needed a healthcare proxy. He turned to leave, but Janice immediately asked for his fax number and informed him that he would get the documents.

Do you know of any couple who travels with a healthcare proxy? If Janice and Lisa were a man and a woman, would anybody have asked for any documents? Would anybody have to ask, even if the couple were not married, to be allowed in the room with each other?

Janice and Lisa had their healthcare power of attorney, living wills, and advanced directives documents drawn up in 2001, shortly after Janice was diagnosed with multiple sclerosis. They tucked the documents away, never envisioning they would need them until they were much older. On that day, Lisa was only thirty-nine years old. Janice, a trained trauma and emergency department social worker, ensured that the couple kept their healthcare proxy and decision-making documents up to date.

Janice wondered in that moment at Ryder Trauma center why their love and commitment of eighteen years was not recognized. With no time to think about such injustice, she jumped into action and called a trusted friend, who rushed to the couple's house, faxed the decision-making documents to Ryder Trauma Center, and called Janice just after 4:20 p.m. to check that the fax was received at the hospital—just forty minutes after Lisa's arrival from the ship.

All of Janice's pleas to find out Lisa's condition or to speak to medical personnel went unanswered despite that the hospital had received the healthcare power of attorney. Janice watched as other families, some with young children, were escorted back through locked doors to see their loved ones while Janice's and their children's anguish increased with every minute that passed.

With papers in hand, Janice would be informed, one would think, of Lisa's medical condition, even in an antigay city and state. At 6:00 p.m.—two and half hours after their arrival—Janice was faced with a decision that would change their family forever. Surgeons informed her that Lisa was nearly brain dead and they needed to know if they should proceed with surgery. Even if Lisa survived the surgery, she would live in a persistent vegetative state. Without even seeing her, Janice was forced to make the decision to follow Lisa's wishes of donating her organs. After the surgeons left, Janice was alone to tell the children that their other mom was going to heaven.

Over the next five and a half hours, Janice begged and pleaded to see Lisa and bring their children to the room to say goodbye. She resorted to showing the children's birth certificates, which listed both of them as mothers, to the desk clerk in an attempt to establish that the children were in fact Lisa's children. They were still not allowed to see their mother.

Janice requested a Catholic priest to administer Lisa's last rites. It was only then that she was given one opportunity to see Lisa for only five minutes.

After 11:30 p.m., when Janice and the children had waited eight hours in the hospital waiting room, Lisa's sister arrived after driving from her home in Jacksonville, Florida. Janice led Lisa's sister inside and brought her to the same desk clerk who worked there all night. Lisa's sister simply stated, "I'm Lisa Pond's sister, and I am here to see her." She was informed that Lisa was moved an hour earlier to the neuro ICU and was given the room number. Lisa's sister was not asked for identification or any paperwork proving her family relationship.

Lisa Pond died of a brain aneurysm at age thirty-nine on February 19, 2007, in Jackson Memorial Hospital. Her children and the love of her life, Janice Langbehn, were a few feet away—but in another room without being able to be with Lisa in her final moments.

Without being able to touch her. Without being able to kiss her goodbye. Without being able to say, "I love you" for the final time.

This is a true story. All the information is factual. That this cruel story happened in Miami, a city that has prospered from gay tourism, tells you that it can happen anywhere.

Janice Langbehn sued the hospital. The judge dismissed the case, despite stating that the hospital "exhibited a lack of compassion and was unbecoming of a renowned trauma center like Ryder [Jackson Memorial Hospital Trauma Center]. Unfortunately, no relief is available for these failures based on the allegations pleaded in the amended complaint."

In other words, there was nothing to sue about because no law had been broken. Hospital visitation discrimination like this was allowed in Florida and other states until January 18, 2011, when new regulations came into effect at the urging of President Obama after learning of the Langbehn-Pond story.

Lisa and Janice, together for eighteen years, parents of four children whom nobody else wanted, were cruelly denied a basic human need: To have your loved ones next to you when you die. In Janice's words, "Holding Lisa's hand is not a *gay* right but a *human* right."

4.

Your Family's Values

Family is very personal, and how you raise your family is up to you. As a father and mother said: "We don't want others to impose *their* family values on our family."

It is all about *your family's* values. For example, this father and mother's family values are clear: They have two daughters, Jackie and Debbie. One daughter is lesbian; the other is not. Taking turns, the parents both said, "Our family's values are that we treat our two daughters the same. We teach them the same ethics and values. We want them to have the same opportunities. We want them to be happy in their lives and one day to marry someone they love and start their own families. We treat our two daughters equally and expect the government to do the same. These are our family's values."

One day recently, this family found out that they held a prejudice that they had not previously realized. They encouraged their non-lesbian daughter, Jackie, to bring her boyfriend home for dinner (but not stay overnight) to ensure that he could get to know the family and vice versa. However, they were uncomfortable asking Debbie to bring her girlfriend.

The parents said: "We did not realize that we were treating our two daughters differently and that we could cause harm that way. Now we check everything we do as parents, to show both our daughters that we love them equally and unconditionally. And it is fine for our daughter Debbie to bring her girlfriend for dinner and family outings—but neither of our daughters gets to bring a boyfriend or girlfriend overnight." The parents and daughters laughed together as they recounted the story.

On a totally different case, here is a true letter from a father to his daughter Christine:
(www.examiner.com/article/dad-disowns-daughter-over-gay-grandson-read-the-viral-letter-here)

Dear Christine:

I'm disappointed in you as a daughter. You are correct that we have "shame in the family," but mistaken about what it is.

Kicking Chad out of your house simply because he told you he was gay is the "abomination" here. A parent disowning her child is what goes "against nature."

The only intelligent think I heard you saying in all this was "you did not raise your son to be gay." Of course, you didn't. He was born this way and didn't choose it more than he being left-handed. You, however, have made a choice of being hurtful, narrow-minded and backward. So, while we are in the business of disowning our children, I think I'll take this moment to say goodbye to you. I now have a fabulous (as the gays put it) grandson to raise, and I do not have time for heartless B-word of a daughter.

If you find your heart, give us a call.

—Dad

These cases highlight examples of good and bad parenting. In fact, research by the Family Acceptance Project of San Francisco State University (familyproject.sfsu.edu) shows the following:

- Suicide attempts by LGBT youth who have high rejection from their family are more than *eight times* the attempts in families with low rejection for their LGBT children.

- Illegal drug use by LGBT youth who experience high rejection from their family is more than *three times* the use for those in families with low rejection for their LGBT children.

- Similarly, the risk of HIV infection is more than *three times* for LGBT youth in families with a high rejection for them.

- Yet another important statistic: 92 percent of LGBT youth in a family that is highly accepting believe that they can be a happy LGBT adult, while only 35 percent of those in a family that is not accepting believe it so.

Several religious leaders are working with the Family Acceptance Project because these scientific findings have opened their minds that tough love can be very detrimental to the health (and survival) of young LGBT people.

Each person is entitled to his or her faith. You may believe that LGBT people will not go to heaven. Other people believe in an all-loving God and that a good person (whether gay or non-gay) will go to heaven. Every parent knows that *love for a child must be unconditional*, in good times and in bad.

There are several parental behaviors that increase the risk of LGBT children developing health and mental problems. These parental behaviors are determined to be unhealthy based not on opinion but on scientific research by the Family Acceptance Project. Here are nine behaviors to avoid:

1. "Hitting, slapping or physically hurting your child because of their LGBT identity."

2. "Verbal harassment or name-calling because of your child's LGBT identity."

3. "Excluding LGBT youth from family and family identity."

4. "Blocking access to LGBT friends, events and resources."

5. "Blaming your child when they are discriminated against because of their LGBT identity."

6. "Pressuring your child to be more (or less) masculine or feminine."

7. "Telling your children that God will punish them because they are gay."

8. "Telling your child that you are ashamed of them or that how they look or act will shame the family."

9. "Making your child keep their LGBT identity a secret in the family and not letting them talk about it."

All parents want the best for their children. When parents decide what's best for their children, they draw on experiences with their parents (good or bad) and all the other experiences from which they have learned throughout their lives. However, most parents have no experience dealing with LGBT children; so, they may respond based on ideas of tough love instead of responses proven to work. Fortunately, research conducted by the Family Acceptance Project shows parental behaviors that can be most helpful to their LGBT children. These recommendations are not based on opinions or beliefs, but on research. Here are eleven things to do:

1. "Talk with your child or foster child about their LGBT identity."

2. "Express affection when your child tells you or when you learn that your child is gay or transgender."

3. "Support your child's LGBT identity even though you may feel uncomfortable."

4. "Advocate for your child when he or she is mistreated because of their LGBT identity."

5. "Require that other family members respect your LGBT child."

6. "Bring your child to LGBT organizations or events."

7. "Talk with your clergy and help your faith community to support LGBT people."

8. "Connect your child with an LGBT adult role model to show them options for the future."

9. "Welcome your child's LGBT friends and partners to your home."

10. "Support your child's gender expression."

11. "Believe your child can have a happy future as an LGBT adult."

This scientific research is opening up many minds—teaching parents to understand the unintended consequences of their past behavior.

For religious parents, this may appear like a conflict, especially when some churches say that homosexuality is an abomination. However, more and more religious leaders are reaching out after understanding the science—and more Christian parents accept what Jesus has always taught: *Unconditional love and commitment*, which is the basis of marriage and of having children. Good parents always want to protect their children from harm.

If you are conflicted about loving your child because he is LGBT, read the blog JustBecauseHeBreathes.com written by a couple who are conservative evangelical parents. Do not miss the letter from the father to his gay son, Ryan. Also, watch the videos by the Family Acceptance Project: FamilyProject.sfsu.edu/family-videos

In summary, you decide your family's values.

What, then, is the definition of a family?

5.

Defining *Family*

In the prior chapters we have met two families: one a non-traditional but sanctified union, the other with more traditional parents but daughters of different sexual orientations.

How *does* one then define a family? Traditionalists have a clear answer: Mother + father + children. This is *their* definition of family. What's *your* definition for *your* family?

As an example, here is the definition that Baptist Health South Florida has for a family (in their 2011 *Outcomes*—a compilation of articles from their Center for Performance Excellence):

> The word *family* triggers images of different "support groups" for each of us. Over time, the "social support group" to us changes, shifts, or expands throughout our lives.
>
> At Baptist Health, each patient defines those individuals who are most important to them—who they view as "family." We recognize and value the importance of these individuals in the healing process. These people may include, but are not limited to, family, friends, and/or other support persons, such as a spouse, a domestic partner (including same-sex domestic partner), other relatives, neighbors, coworkers or clergy. **In other words, each patient has the right to define who can be present and participate in their care and visitation.**

The bold typeface is in the original article. Note that Baptist Health South Florida is a *faith-based* healthcare organization ranking at the top in the United States. They understand the definition of a family since they see patients constantly defining who their families are.

There are more stories about families in the book *Ties that Bind* by Dave Isay.

Each of us knows who our true family is: The people we turn to when we are most in need. How have we come to allow others to impose a definition of who should be our families?

This is an attack on our personal freedom.

People use several arguments to deny others' freedoms. Let's examine these arguments one by one in the next chapters.

6.

It's Unnatural!

Some people think that homosexual, bisexual, and transgender people are mentally sick, that what they do is unnatural, and that the Bible says it is an abomination. These beliefs serve as a justification for people to discriminate, such as to deny a family the right to be together when the mother was dying at a hospital, as we saw in Chapter 3.

Would God accept the behavior of the people in that hospital in Miami who did not allow Lisa's partner to be next to her as she was dying? What about their young children, who had nothing to do with their parents' sexual orientation?

Let's discuss now one of the most common arguments used to discriminate: that homosexuality is a sin against nature.

To see if it is true, we need to check whether homosexuality and bisexuality exist in animals in nature.

Evidence is very clear that animals exhibit homosexual and bisexual behaviors. Here are just a few examples from Wikipedia: (en.wikipedia.org/wiki/Homosexual_behavior_in_animals)

- *Giraffes:* about nine out of ten matings occur between males.

- *Domesticated sheep:* about 10 percent of males do not mate with females—only males.

- *Black swans:* about 25 percent of the matings are between males. Male couples also raise young black swans.

- *Western gulls:* 10 to 15 percent of females show homosexual behavior.

- *Wild ducks:* about 19 percent of all pairings are male with male.

- *Penguins:* many male-to-male long-term relationships have been reported, including building nests together.

- *Vultures:* bisexual vultures have been studied in zoos.

- *Pigeons:* male-male and female-female relationships have been documented. Same-gender couples build nests together.

- *American bisons:* same-sex relationships are documented as common.

- *Bonobos (apes):* they are considered a bisexual species (60 percent of sexual activity is between two or more females).

- *Dolphins:* there is well-reported bisexual behavior, especially among bottlenose dolphins.

- *Elephants:* there is well-documented bisexual behavior, with stronger bonds between males.

- *Lions:* about 8 percent of mountings are male-male.

- *Spotted hyena:* have strong female-to-female relationships.

- *Lizards:* females can take masculine or feminine sexual roles.

- *Dragonflies:* high incidence of mating among males.

This article concludes, *"No species has been found in which homosexual behavior has not been shown to exist, except for species that never have sex at all."* Therefore, we cannot say that homosexuality and bisexuality are unnatural when they are present in nature.

Furthermore, a phenomena similar to intersex occurs in nature in which organisms have both male and female characteristics. It is called gynandromorphism and has been documented in butterflies, lobsters, crabs, and birds such as northern cardinals.

Some people would say, "Fine, we cannot say that it is unnatural, but these people are mentally sick." The next chapter responds to this pronouncement.

7.

You Are Sick!

Given the scientific evidence, we need to agree that homosexuality and bisexuality occur naturally in animals. What about in humans? Has this topic been studied by science? The answer is yes. Research by psychologists like Alfred Kinsey, Magnus Hirschfeld, and Sigmund Freud, among others, shows that sexual orientation appears as a spectrum from totally heterosexual to bisexual to totally homosexual.

Repeated studies show that people fall into different parts of the spectrum of sexual orientation. This is a natural phenomenon, same as for handedness which falls also into a continuous spectrum: most people are right-handed, some are left-handed, and some are ambidextrous.

The American Psychological Association confirms:
(www.apa.org/helpcenter/sexual-orientation.aspx)

> Both heterosexual behavior and homosexual behavior are normal aspects of human sexuality. Both have been documented in many different cultures and historical eras. Despite the persistence of stereotypes that portray lesbian, gay, and bisexual people as disturbed, several decades of research and clinical experience have led all mainstream medical and mental health organizations in this country to conclude that these orientations represent normal forms of human experience. Lesbian, gay, and bisexual relationships are normal forms of human bonding. Therefore, these mainstream organizations long ago abandoned classifications of homosexuality as a mental disorder.

Clearly, scientific organizations have concluded that homosexuality, heterosexuality, and bisexuality are normal forms of the human experience and that they are not mental disorders.

We cannot say that homosexuality is unnatural since it occurs in nature. Furthermore, we cannot say that people with a homosexual sexual orientation are sick since it has been proven scientifically not to be the case.

But, you may say, the Bible says homosexuality is an abomination. You are right on this one—read on.

8.

The Bible Says So

"The same Bible that teaches us about the virtue of chastity and fidelity in marriage also teaches us not to judge people."

—Cardinal Timothy M. Dolan, May 24, 2014

We have already seen that we cannot call homosexuality unnatural since it is well documented that it happens in nature. Nor can we say that homosexuality is a disease since for several decades the American Psychological Association and other organizations have clearly stated that it is a normal aspect of human sexuality.

So, it's not unnatural, and it is not a disease. However, some people believe that, based on what the Bible says, homosexuality is an abomination.

Indeed, Leviticus 18:22 (King James Version) clearly says, "Thou shalt not lie with mankind, as with womankind: It is an abomination." Some experts contend that the term *abomination* is mistranslated. However, since religion is based on personal faith, we should respect those who take the meaning literally.

Furthermore, Leviticus 20:13 (King James Version) establishes the death penalty for homosexual acts:

> If a man also lie with mankind, as he lieth with a woman, both of them have committed an abomination: they shall surely be put to death; their blood shall be upon them.

If you are willing to accept that homosexual acts are an abomination subject to the death penalty then you have to accept the penalty that the same chapter of Leviticus establishes:

Leviticus 20:9 For every one that curseth his father or his mother shall be surely put to death: he hath cursed his father or his mother; his blood shall be upon him.

Leviticus 20:10 And the man that committeth adultery with another man's wife, even he that committeth adultery with his neighbour's wife, the adulterer and the adulteress shall surely be put to death.

Leviticus 20:11 And the man that lieth with his father's wife hath uncovered his father's nakedness: both of them shall surely be put to death; their blood shall be upon them.

Leviticus 20:12 And if a man lie with his daughter in law, both of them shall surely be put to death: they have wrought confusion; their blood shall be upon them.

Leviticus 20:13 If a man also lie with mankind, as he lieth with a woman, both of them have committed an abomination: they shall surely be put to death; their blood shall be upon them.

Leviticus 20:14 And if a man take a wife and her mother, it is wickedness: they shall be burnt with fire, both he and they; that there be no wickedness among you.

Leviticus 20:15 And if a man lie with a beast, he shall surely be put to death: and ye shall slay the beast.

Leviticus 20:16 And if a woman approach unto any beast, and lie down thereto, thou shalt kill the woman, and the beast: they shall surely be put to death; their blood shall be upon them.

Leviticus 20:17 And if a man shall take his sister, his father's daughter, or his mother's daughter, and see her nakedness, and she see his nakedness; it is a wicked thing; and they shall be cut off in the sight of their people: he hath uncovered his sister's nakedness; he shall bear his iniquity.

Leviticus 20:18 And if a man shall lie with a woman having her sickness, and shall uncover her nakedness; he hath discovered her fountain, and she hath uncovered the fountain of her blood: and both of them shall be cut off from among their people.

Leviticus 20:19 And thou shalt not uncover the nakedness of thy mother's sister, nor of thy father's sister: for he uncovereth his near kin: they shall bear their iniquity.

Leviticus 20:20 And if a man shall lie with his uncle's wife, he hath uncovered his uncle's nakedness: they shall bear their sin; they shall die childless.

Leviticus 20:21 And if a man shall take his brother's wife, it is an unclean thing: he hath uncovered his brother's nakedness; they shall be childless.

So if you curse your father or mother, you should be put to death. And if you commit adultery with a married woman, both of you should be put to death. So if you believe that homosexual acts are an abomination that results in the perpetrators deserving to be put to death then you should be consistent with the other commandments in the same chapter of Leviticus. There are more commandments in Leviticus:

Leviticus 11:10–12 And all that have not fins and scales in the seas, and in the rivers, of all that move in the waters, and of any living thing which is in the waters, they shall be an abomination unto you. They shall be even an abomination unto you; ye shall not eat of their flesh, but ye shall have their carcasses in abomination. Whatsoever hath no fins nor scales in the waters, that shall be an abomination unto you.

So, not only are homosexual acts an abomination but eating shrimp and other fish without fins is an abomination, too. The point is not to debate or contest *your* interpretation of the Bible. Some Christians believe that the translation may not consider the context of the times and the exact meaning of the words. Other Christians believe that the Bible should be read literally; if this is your belief, please act consistently by choosing what you cannot eat and lobby to establish the death penalty not only for homosexual acts but also for the heterosexual acts listed in Leviticus.

The point here is not to change your religious beliefs but to encourage you to be *consistent* with them. In fact, it is very important to respect and protect the freedom of religion, as the next chapter attests.

9.

Your Freedom of Religion

"A gay person who is seeking God, who is of good
will—well, who am I to judge him?"

—Pope Francis, July 28, 2013

Clearly, in a civilized society, we are not going to execute men who commit adultery with married women, just as we are not going to execute people who have romantic relationships with a person of the same gender. Similarly, in a civilized society, we are not going to call people with a homosexual sexual orientation an abomination but remain silent about people who commit the abomination, per Leviticus 11, of eating shrimp or any shellfish.

Fortunately, most Americans want to respect each other's freedom of religion. It is true: Some religions do believe that homosexual acts should be penalized and that indeed people with a homosexual sexual orientation should not be treated equally under the law. However, some other religions differ; they believe that every person is a child of God, loved by God, and should be treated equally.

Some people, however, work hard to attack the freedom of religion. In January 2013, the National Cathedral, which is the second largest church in the United States and part of the Episcopal faith, announced that it will marry people of the same gender. A month after that decision, the Faith and Freedom Coalition, an organization founded by conservative Ralph Reed, demanded "an immediate suspension of any current or future federal funds to this institution." So much for their belief in freedom of religion.

How do we go about protecting freedom of religion?

We should protect the freedom of each religion, since we can only protect your freedom of religion if we protect others' freedom of religion. If your religion believes that homosexuality is an abomination and does not allow people of the same gender to marry, it is fine. If your religion accepts people with a homosexual sexual orientation and their right to marry, fine, too. The government should not impose on any religion whom to marry (or divorce) or, for that matter, force any religion to have bishops who are female or LGBT.

Government cannot impose one religion's views on another. This is why each religion is regulated by its own laws and civic life by its own laws. Americans cherish the requirement expressed in the US Constitution:

> Congress shall make no law respecting an establishment of religion, or prohibiting the free exercise thereof.

A factor in the greatness of our country comes from having freedom of religion; that is, you can follow any religion you wish without the government imposing a religion on you or creating laws based on a religion. You do not want our laws to be based on Sharia law, or Jewish law, Catholic law, Baptist law or any other faith. Every individual is free to follow the law of his or her church, while the government creates and enforces civil laws.

The New Mexico Supreme Court said it eloquently in their marriage equality decision on December 19, 2013: "Our analysis does not and cannot depend on religious doctrine without violating the Constitution."

Still, some people say that our *civil* laws should not treat people with a homosexual orientation equally because homosexuality is a choice. But, is it a choice?

The next chapter tackles this important question.

10.

Is Homosexuality a Choice?

"If I was gay I wouldn't hide it. Being gay or straight
isn't bad or good it just IS. U are who you are.
Be true to yourself.

— Ansel Elgort, December 18, 2014

Sexual orientation defines our attraction to other people. By definition, sexual orientation can be heterosexual (attracted to people of a different gender), homosexual (attracted to people of the same gender), or bisexual (attracted to people of either gender).

So the question is: is sexual orientation a choice?

Ask this question to yourself. Is *your* sexual orientation a choice? If you answer yes, when did you choose your sexual orientation? How did you make that choice?

Or, more pointedly, for heterosexuals: When did you decide to be a heterosexual? Did you decide you were heterosexual even before you had sex? Did you always know because you were just born that way? Did it just come naturally?

Certainly, most readers have answered no—meaning that sexual orientation was not a choice for them. Bisexual individuals may answer that at some point they were attracted to one gender and at some other point in their lives to the other or that they were equally attracted to both.

If your child tells you that he or she is gay or lesbian or bisexual or transgender, do not blame yourself. *You did nothing wrong*. You did not influence him or her to be LGBT, nor did your parents influence you to be a heterosexual, just as homosexual parents cannot influence their children to be LGBT. It is the way it is.

There is growing research that the sexual orientation of the parents—heterosexual, homosexual, or bisexual—does not affect the orientation of the children they raise.

The people who believe that homosexuality is a choice use this to deny people with a different sexual orientation or gender identity equal protection under the law. They claim that the law should protect against discrimination because of race, gender, or national origin because those factors are obviously not a choice.

Here is the catch: While the law protects against discrimination based on non-choice characteristics such as race, gender, and national origin, it also protects *religion*—which is clearly a personal choice. So you cannot fairly say that it is okay to discriminate against gays because being gay is a choice. Even if homosexuality were a choice, which it is not, it should be protected against discrimination.

There is yet another argument that some people still use to justify discrimination against gay, lesbian, bisexual, and transgender people. They say it can be cured. Let's consider this question in the next chapter.

11.

Let *Me* Straighten *You*

If your sexual orientation is heterosexual, do you think that with therapy you could become homosexual?

You are very likely to answer: *"No way. Nobody would be able to make me homosexual. And I do not want to change anyway."*

Indeed, most people do not want to change something as intrinsic as their sexual orientation, whether they are heterosexual, homosexual, or bisexual.

However, there is heavy societal pressure to be part of the majority. So whether because of their religion, or not knowing that sexual orientation falls naturally into a spectrum, or fear of rejection by society, some people still struggle with their sexual orientation. They try to change their sexual orientation to heterosexual and "be cured." Some families, for similar reasons, bring their children to therapy (called reparative or conversion therapy) to "make them straight."

As hard as it might be to believe for those who think that homosexuality is an abomination, there is nothing to be cured.

The most important study on the subject was conducted in 2001 by Robert Spitzer, MD, a well-respected professor of psychiatry at Columbia University. Dr. Spitzer addressed the issue of whether individuals could change their sexual orientation from homosexual to heterosexual using reparative or conversation therapy. He concluded that *some* highly motivated individuals could do it. The report was published in the *Archives of Sexual Behavior* but was not peer-reviewed, a critical requirement for any scientific work. Eventually, Dr. Spitzer concluded that his research was fundamentally flawed, and that there was no evidence that reparative therapy worked because statements from participants about their self-evaluation of the success of such therapy could not be relied upon.

This is what the American Psychological Association has to say regarding therapies to change sexual orientation: (www.apa.org/helpcenter/sexual-orientation.aspx)

> To date, there has been no scientifically adequate research to show that therapy aimed at changing sexual orientation (sometimes called reparative or conversion therapy) is safe or effective. Furthermore, it seems likely that the promotion of change therapies reinforces stereotypes and contributes to a negative climate for lesbian, gay, and bisexual persons. This appears to be especially likely for lesbian, gay, and bisexual individuals who grow up in more conservative religious settings.

So there is no evidence that such therapies are safe or effective.

The most prominent organization involved in so-called reparative or conversion therapy is Exodus International. In an interesting twist, Michael Bussee, one of its cofounders, left the organization in 1979 to live together with another cofounder of Exodus, Gary Cooper. To go even further, they had a commitment ceremony in 1982 (well before civil unions or marriage equality existed).

Years later, in October 2000, the chair of Exodus International, John Paulk, was removed from his position after being spotted drinking and flirting at a gay bar in Washington, DC.

More recently, in 2011, John Smid, the former executive director of Love in Action (another organization that claimed to "straighten homosexuals"), said, "I never met a man who experienced a change from homosexual to heterosexual."

Putting a final nail to this coffin, Alan Chambers, the president of Exodus International, said in June 2012 that "there was no cure for homosexuality and that 'reparative therapy' offered false hopes to gays and could even be harmful."

So it doesn't work.

Finally, after forty years, Exodus International closed its doors in 2013. Its president, Alan Chambers, stated:

> Exodus is an institution in the conservative Christian world, but we've ceased to be a living, breathing organism. For quite some time we've been imprisoned in a worldview that's neither honoring toward our fellow human beings, nor biblical.

On April 24, 2013, the former chair of Exodus International, John Paulk stated:

> Please allow me to be clear: I do not believe that reparative therapy changes sexual orientation; in fact, it does great harm to people.

Despite such clear statements, other organizations continue to try to straighten LGBT people. Such an organization is Courage, a Catholic apostolate. There's a twist: Paul Scalia, a priest who is the son of virulently antigay, the late Supreme Court Justice Scalia, works there.

A very good resource and an organization worth supporting is Truth Wins Out (truthwinsout.org). This organization specializes in debunking the ex-gay myth and counters disinformation campaigns about LGBT people. Its founder, Wayne Besen, is the author of *Anything but Straight: Unmasking the Scandals and Lies Behind the Ex-Gay Myth*. It is a book worth reading if you want to know more about this topic.

In May 2015, congressman Ted Lieu (D-CA) introduced the Therapeutic Fraud Prevention Act that prohibits reparative therapy and marketing of it for compensation. It has 68 cosponsors in the House and it has not been introduced in the Senate yet. This legislation is also supported by President Obama.

Some people may say, "Okay, I accept gays but please do not flaunt it." This concern is addressed in the following chapter.

12.

Don't Flaunt It

Some people say they can *tolerate* people who are gay, lesbian, bisexual, or transgender—but they add: "Just don't flaunt it." These people think that not "flaunting" sexual orientation, or hiding it, is a good compromise. In reality, this so-called compromise is harming (albeit unintentionally) LGBT people.

An important part of a healthy mind is to be able to be who you are. This was a main argument expressed by the Chairman of the Joint Chiefs of Staff, Admiral Mullen, in support of the repeal of "Don't Ask, Don't Tell": it is *immoral* to force people to lie about and hide who they are.

Furthermore, a civilized society means that we respect other people—not just *tolerate* them. For instance, many years ago, the World Jewish Congress changed its vocabulary from "tolerance" to "respect."

It is wonderful to see a couple holding hands and showing their love. It is a public demonstration of commitment, love, and caring. It is wonderful independent of the gender of the couple. Notice that we are talking about public displays of affection—not about having sex in public (which is not appropriate whether the couple is same gender or different gender).

But what about the children? Some people say, "I do not want my children to see a homosexual couple. It is bad for the kids" believing that it will make their children homosexual. Of course, this is not true: If you are heterosexual, can you fathom for a second that you would have become homosexual just by seeing a same-gender couple holding hands when you were a child? Let's be real.

In reality, you may be causing harm to your children if they see you reacting negatively about a same-gender couple's public display of affection. The message that you are sending is that homosexuality is wrong and that you may not love your children if they are homosexual. Seeing a same-gender public display of affection is an opportunity for you to teach the importance of understanding for, acceptance of, and respect for other human beings—and to let your children know that you will still love them even if they are homosexual or bisexual or transgender. Because you *will* still love them—won't you?

For those interested in the science, here is what the American Psychological Association has to say: (www.apa.org/helpcenter/sexual-orientation.aspx)

> Sexual orientation is commonly discussed as if it were solely a characteristic of an individual, like biological sex, gender identity, or age. This perspective is incomplete because sexual orientation is defined in terms of relationships with others. People express their sexual orientation through behaviors with others, including such simple actions as holding hands or kissing. Thus, sexual orientation is closely tied to the intimate personal relationships that meet deeply felt needs for love, attachment, and intimacy. In addition to sexual behaviors, these bonds include nonsexual physical affection between partners, shared goals and values, mutual support, and ongoing commitment. Therefore, sexual orientation is not merely a personal characteristic within an individual. Rather, one's sexual orientation defines the group of people in which one is likely to find the satisfying and fulfilling romantic relationships that are an essential component of personal identity for many people.

So, it is about flaunting it. The freedom to be yourself is a part of one's sexual orientation and gender identity and expression and is a necessary component of a healthy lifestyle. It is about the freedom and respect to be yourself and have your individuality.

Some people get it—check the next chapter.

13.

Understand, Accept, and Respect

More than thirty years ago, a young man, proud of being the big man in high school, started his first day of college to discover that he had been assigned a gay roommate. He was surprised but accepted it. After their freshman year, their lives took different paths. This young man ended up on Wall Street and was by the Twin Towers on September 11, 2001. Thankfully, he survived.

Life continued, and when President Obama announced his support for the freedom to marry, this young man e-mailed his freshman roommate of more than thirty years ago:

> With the President coming out and making a statement on same sex marriage I reference you often. I speak that you and I still stay in touch after all these years and that you were the first person to contact me after 9/11. I will always remember that. I have you and your friends to thank for enabling me to understand, accept and respect gay people. Being 18 and big man on campus in HS, if you were going to tell me that my college roommate would be gay, I would have said you're crazy. Just another example of not judging a book by its cover. It's wonderful that the time we were roommates has left a lasting impact on me.
>
> Thanks again.
>
> Be well.

Understand, accept, and respect.

That's all that needs to be said.

14.

I Need To Go To The Bathroom!

Choosing which public bathroom to use is a simple decision that we make without much thought since we follow a simple social convention: if you identify as a man, you go to the men's room and if you identify as a woman you go to the ladies' room. That simple.

Now some Republican state legislatures want to regulate to which bathroom you go based on your gender at birth. You may be transitioning, having been born a woman but already dressing as a male. So these legislators want you to go to the ladies' room... imagine the eyebrows this would raise! While if you look like a man and go to the men's room nobody will care or check if you have a penis. This is what people have been doing forever without any problems.

Proving that legislators are capable of creating insane regulations, in some conservative states they are proposing to give cash rewards to vigilantes who would uncover people going to the wrong bathroom. What will they do? Detain you until they can verify your gender at birth? How are they going to prove it? Will they require a visual inspection of your organs?

Trying to find cover, these legislators say that they do not want people of different genders in the same bathroom as rapes or molestation could occur. But those crimes are already well covered in existing legislation, and if somebody wants to enter the other gender's bathroom to commit a crime, they can do it at any time, independently of these new bathroom regulations.

The legislature of North Carolina become notorious in March 2016 when in just 12 hours they introduced their bathroom bill (HB2), discussed it in the two chambers and got it signed by the governor. This rushed-through legislation also forbade the use of state courts for cases of race and gender discrimination and forbade cities and counties for having non-discrimination legislation or minimum wage higher than the state. This is a dream come through: pass all these regressive measures and limit the autonomy of cities and counties in less than 12 hours. For a Republican party that prides itself of autonomy for the state and local government, it was quite a reversal.

Here is a letter written by a 9th grader to the governor of North Carolina regarding the bathroom law, HB2:

Dear Governor McCrory:

My name is Skye Thomson. I am 15 years old, I live in Eastern North Carolina, and I am a transgender boy. That means I was born a female and identify as a male.

I was in Raleigh for the debate on House Bill 2 on March 23. I was the only transgender student who got a chance to speak out against HB2, the so called "bathroom bill" that is supposed to keep everyone safe in bathrooms. But it doesn't keep everyone safe, especially people like me. Imagine yourself in my shoes, being a boy walking into a ladies room. It's awkward and embarrassing and can actually be dangerous. By putting this law in place you're putting kids like me in danger.

I've dealt with bullying my whole life. And now I feel that my own state lawmakers and governor are bullying me as well. I face daily harassment for being myself, everything from dirty looks to physical assaults. I don't report them because I know it will just make the other kids bully me more. In schools all over the place transgender kids go through the same thing every day. Because of the constant harassment, I have had more than one transgender friend attempt suicide.

HB2 just gives other students all the more reason to hate us.

After my speech at the HB2 hearing, two people from your staff invited me to a private meeting. They said that you wanted to learn more about the difficulties transgender kids like me face. At the end of our meeting, I asked your staff if I could meet with you in person before you made your decision about HB2. I hoped that if we met you would see that I'm just like any other kid, a kid worth protecting. I wanted to tell you my story, really bad things that have happened to me that I'm not comfortable sharing in this letter and that should never happen to a kid. Your staff said they would try to find a way for us to meet, but we never did. You signed HB2 into law an hour later.

Governor, I would still like to meet with you if at all possible. My friends would like to meet with you too. We think that if you get to know us, you will work on helping to keep us safe in bathrooms and everywhere else we go.

Thank you for your time,

Skye Thomson, 9th Grader

A transgender man in North Carolina when using a ladies' room (as he is required now by this law) distributes a card that says:

My name is Charlie.

I'm following the law that was passed on March 23rd. I am a transgender man who would be rather using the men's room right now.

This is likely uncomfortable for both of us.

Please contact your legislature and tell them you oppose HB2.

Or as another North Carolina transgender man twitted to the governor: "It's now the law for me to share a restroom with your wife."

To legislate effectively requires thoughtfulness, understanding, and restrain. None of these characteristics were present in North Carolina.

Obviously, stupidity in regulations has no limits. A simple decision like going to the bathroom can become an ordeal in some states for every one.

15.

You're the Wife!

In December 2015, the archbishop of Santo Domingo, Dominican Republic, said about the US Ambassador to his country: "Let him focus on housework, since he is the wife to a man."

It is incredible that a high official of a country would make such a remark about the highest foreign official representing the United States. The archbishop declared that the role of women is to do housework. That by itself would be a highly inappropriate public comment.

It gets even more inappropriate: Ambassador Wally Brewster, to whom the comments were addressed, is openly gay and legally married to Robert Satawake.

So, it seems that the archbishop not only likes to degrade women, but also wants to assume who is the "wife" in a gay relationship.

The next chapter addresses the assumptions people make about the roles in same-gender relationships.

16.

Are You the Wife?

With the ruling by the US Supreme Court in June 2015 that the Constitution grants to couples of the same gender the fundamental right to get married, more people are trying to understand what role each of the spouses plays. Who's the wife? Who's the husband?

Marriage traditionalists are keen on marriage being between one man and one woman and they also claim that children need a father and a mother. These are all code words to imply that fathers and mothers have different roles that the children need to be educated about and continue to honor. For these traditionalists, fathers are supposed to be assertive and head of the households, while mothers need to be nurturing and take care of the children and house chores. Some religions expect the wife to be submissive to the husband. This is why they view same-gender marriage as such a threat, as they cannot establish who is now the husband and who is the wife.

Fortunately, more and more heterosexual couples understand that the roles that each of them play in a marriage depend on their personality, interests, skills, time availability, and other factors instead of their gender. They understand that they are equals in their marriage.

It is likely that you know, or soon you will know, a married couple of the same gender. How do you address them? Definitely, do not call them "friends," or "boyfriends," or "partners." We are well past those times. Pay attention to the terms they use. Most married male couples will introduce themselves as husbands. So they will say: "This is my husband Ken" and the other will say "this is my husband Juan." This has no implication about household chores or sexual activity. And, of course, do not try to assume roles by asking "who cooks?" or "who cleans?" They may tell you who cooked that delicious dinner when you were at their house. Next time the cook may be the other person.

While husbands is the term used more frequently among male couples, you may find some female couples apprehensive about using the term wives for each other, because it connotes to them a discriminated role. So, just pay attention about how they address each other.

In case of doubt, use the term "spouses" which is appropriate for any married couple, whether homosexual or heterosexual.

17.

Supreme Words

"Equal Justice Under Law"

—Inscription in the façade of the US Supreme Court
building

The US Supreme Court ruled on June 26, 2015 that same sex couples had the right to marry nationwide. Here are some quotes from that historic decision. May we all take these words to heart:

Held: The Fourteenth Amendment requires a State to license a marriage between two people of the same sex and to recognize a marriage between two people of the same sex when their marriage was lawfully licensed and performed out-of-State. [...]

Sexual orientation is both a normal expression of human sexuality and immutable. [...]

The nature of marriage is that, through its enduring bond, two persons together can find other freedoms, such as expression, intimacy, and spirituality. This is true for all persons, whatever their sexual orientation. [...]

There is dignity in the bond between two men or two women who seek to marry and in their autonomy to make such profound choices. [...]

Same-sex couples have the same right as opposite-sex couples to enjoy intimate association. [...]

Under the Constitution, same-sex couples seek in marriage the same legal treatment as opposite-sex couples, and it would disparage their choices and

diminish their personhood to deny them this right.
[...]

In summary, the US Constitution gives the same marriage rights to all couples independently of gender.

18.

It's about Personal Freedom; It's about Being Better People

> "The claim that same-sex marriage is destroying society is actually greatly overstated. Christians who themselves abandoned the primacy of lifelong marriage to follow the divorce and remarriage customs of a secular society have as much to answer for as those who militantly push to redefine marriage."
>
> —Mike Huckabee, 2014 in *God, Guns, Grits and Gravy*

The essence of personal freedom is to live and let live. For you to be free means that others need to be free. For example, you are free to follow a religious belief that homosexuality is an abomination. But you have to let others be free to follow their own religious belief that God loves all His creatures equally, including practicing homosexuals.

However, you are not free to cause bodily or psychological harm to others.

You should not stop others from having the same rights as you do or vote against them having the same rights that you have.

So this book is about freedom, as well as being better people.

It's about respecting others' choices—giving them freedom, even if we disagree. You may not want romantic intimacy with somebody of the same gender. However, we should respect and celebrate the fact that two people love each other—even if they are the same gender.

Being better people is about knowing that we are *not judging*. It is not about tolerating others, but about respecting and celebrating their freedom to be unique—maybe very different from you or from the majority but still unique individuals with their virtues and faults, like each of us.

Being a better person, being free and respecting the personal freedom of others, and being treated equally under the law are the fundamental essence that most of us who love our country share.

19.

Summary: Who Are These LGBT People?

In the preceding chapters, we have learned a little bit more about lesbian, gay, bisexual, and transgender individuals. In summary, LGBT people are not alien to our lives. They are our neighbors, paramedics, firefighters, elected officials, military personnel, writers, police officers, business executives, and others in all professions, backgrounds, and locations. They are also people who have made very important contributions to society in the military, the sciences, the arts, business and many other fields.

We have seen that you cannot call homosexuality or bisexuality unnatural since it happens every day in nature. Science also agrees that homosexuality is not a disease and that there is nothing to cure, nor is there any effective method to change an individual's sexual orientation.

We have also seen that although the Bible can be interpreted as saying that homosexual acts are an abomination, not everybody agrees with that interpretation. (But if you do, to be consistent you cannot commit any other abomination, such as eating shrimp.)

Freedom of religion is very important. Since different religions have different religious laws about matters such as marriage, divorce, ordination, role of women, etc., we cannot impose one religion over another when we create *civil laws.*

Further, we've learned that the issue is not whether homosexuality is a choice: religion is clearly a personal choice and is included in all of our nondiscrimination legislation (as it should be).

Finally, we've seen that family values are defined by *each* family. For many families, a most important value is that they want all their children to be treated equally—independent of their sexual orientation or gender identity or expression.

Now that we know who these LGBT people are, it is time to examine the gay agenda. What do lesbian, gay, bisexual, and transgender individuals want? Do they want special rights? These and other questions will be explored in the next chapters.

Part II:

Why A Gay Agenda?

20.

Special Rights

Does anyone deserve special rights?

Think about it. Commit to an answer.

My answer is this: yes, some people deserve special rights.

What?

You got it right: Some people do deserve special rights. Take, for example, a married couple. They get special rights. Here are some of the special rights married couples get:

- Unlimited, tax-free transfer of assets between spouses (including at death)

- Filing taxes jointly

- Making medical decisions for each other and their children

- Survivor Social Security benefits after death of a spouse

- Funeral and bereavement leave

- Ability to file wrongful death claims

- Spousal communications privilege that protects confidential communications between spouses during civil and criminal cases

- Spousal testimonial privilege that allows spouses not to testify against each other in a court of law

- Ability to sponsor the other spouse for immigration to the United States

- Joint adoption and foster care

- Automatic legal status with stepchildren

These are just some of the 1,138 special rights that married people get (per the report of the United States General Accounting Office dated January 23, 2004). Indeed, they should get them.

There are also special rights conferred to some people as protections against discrimination or hate crimes. These special rights are based on characteristics at birth that cannot be changed, such as race, gender, and country of origin. Some of the special protections are based on characteristics that are, and should be, a personal choice, such as choice of religion.

So, LGBT people are not seeking special rights that nobody else receives—just to be treated like people in the same circumstances.

If you are not gay, why should you care about gay rights? You might be surprised by some of the reasons, discussed in the next chapter.

21.

If I Am Not Gay, Why Should I Care about Gay Rights?

You should care because the crucial issue is not about gay rights; it is about who we are as a country and as good human beings. Do we accept the personal freedom of others to be unique individuals? Should anybody have to fear for their lives or their jobs just for being who they are? It is all about basic human rights. It is about the fundamental belief that we all share in America to be treated equally under the law.

Also, you should care if you have young children or grandchildren. They already have a sexual orientation (heterosexual, homosexual, or bisexual), even if they are too young to know it. We have already discussed that conversion therapies do not work. Wouldn't you then want for your children and grandchildren to live in a country in which they are treated equally under the law, independent of their sexual orientation and gender identity and expression?

This is an opportunity for you to speak to others about accepting and embracing family members, coworkers and friends who are lesbian, gay, bisexual or transgender. Your words and actions as a straight ally carry much more weight that if they were uttered by an LGBT person.

Acceptance and equality works both ways. For example, say that you are heterosexual and a great accountant who wants to work for an LGBT organization that provides great benefits and it is close to your home. You should not be discriminated against because of your sexual orientation; you should be able to work for a gay organization. Discrimination based on sexual orientation (heterosexual, homosexual, or bisexual) should not be allowed, and the same goes for gender identity (the gender you identify with) and expression (how you express your gender).

Here's one more example: Imagine you are outside a public restroom holding your girlfriend's purse. You are 100-percent heterosexual, but some thugs think that because you are holding a purse, you are homosexual, and they attack you as they shout, "Faggot! Faggot! Here is what you deserve!" This has actually happened.

Nobody deserves to be a victim of a hate crime. Thanks to legislation passed by Congress and signed into law in 2009 by President Obama, you are protected against hate crimes because of your religion, race, national origin, gender, sexual orientation, gender identity and expression, and disability.

Now that you care about equal rights for everybody, what's the gay agenda? Let's discuss first, a congressman's gay agenda.

22.

Barney Frank's Radical Homosexual Agenda

Barney Frank was, until his retirement in January 2013, the most senior openly gay member of Congress. He was a member of Congress for more than thirty years and was chair of the powerful House Financial Services Committee for four years. He was considered by many to be a very savvy legislator. He is a graduate of Harvard College and Harvard Law School.

On December 22, 2010, four days after Congress repealed "Don't Ask, Don't Tell," Representative Frank addressed, during a press conference, what others called the "Barney Frank radical homosexual agenda." He said that this agenda was:

1. To be protected against violent crimes driven by bigotry

2. To be able to get married

3. To be able to get a job

4. To be able to fight for our country

He added, "For those who are worried about the radical homosexual agenda, let me put them on notice—two down, two to go." As for the "two down," he was referring to the repeal of "Don't Ask, Don't Tell" and the expansion of federal hate-crimes legislation to include sexual orientation and gender identity and expression. The "two to go" referred to the right to get married and to employment nondiscrimination.

As much as he is respected, and as much as his speech was wonderful and punchy, this is not the gay agenda. As the next chapter discusses, we need to think bigger.

23.

Thinking *Bigger*

Congressman Frank's "two down, two to go" should be more like "one and a half down, several more to go."

The "one" that is "down" is the hate-crimes protection that was achieved (at the federal level) when President Obama signed into law the Matthew Shepard and James Byrd, Jr. Hate Crimes Prevention Act on October 28, 2009. Here's a caveat: this legislation, while very useful, is not a replacement for state hate-crimes legislation, which is really needed in each state.

A goal that is half down is for service members serving openly in the military. As we explain in Chapter 31, these service members could still be discriminated against (until 2015 when this was corrected), and transgender service members are still not allowed to serve their country.

In terms of the two to go, Congressman Frank was referring to marriage (which was achieved in 2015) and employment nondiscrimination (still pending). However, there are more than two goals that need to be achieved, including anti-bullying and safety in the schools, parenting rights, and nondiscrimination in housing, financing, public accommodations, and federal government programs.

The LGBT movement, while making significant progress (especially in the states, courts, and public opinion), suffers from not thinking big enough. We saw that Barney Frank's "radical homosexual agenda" was incomplete. For some people, the approach is: *ask for little—get even less.*

So, what's the real gay agenda? The true gay agenda is disclosed in detail in the next chapter.

24.

Q: What's the Gay Agenda?

A: The American Agenda– Equal Treatment under the Law

"The compelling argument is on the side of homosexuals. That's where the compelling argument is: 'We're Americans. We just want to be treated like everybody else.'"

—Bill O'Reilly on Fox News, March 26, 2013

The gay agenda is very simple: Being treated equally under the law, which happens to be the American Agenda. This is the shared belief among Americans that has made us such a great country. It is the Golden Rule of treating others as you want to be treated. It is inscribed in huge letters in the facade of the US Supreme Court building: "Equal Justice Under Law."

To achieve the gay agenda, just look at the laws (federal and state) —whenever you see protections based on race, gender, national origin, and religion, just add the words *sexual orientation* and *gender identity*.

That's it. As Harvey Milk said:

> All men are created equal. No matter how hard you try, you can never erase those words.

If you have read the previous chapters of this book, you know that:

- Nobody is asking for special rights. LGBT people just want to be treated like other groups—no need to create special legislation for us. Just add "sexual orientation and gender identity" to existing legislation.

- Nobody is comparing the suffering of different groups protected under the law. People have suffered tremendous discrimination and prejudice because of their race, and their gender, and their national origin, and their religion, and their disability, and their sexual orientation, and their gender identity.

- Nobody wants to curtail your freedom of religion. Some religions support LGBT equality while others oppose it. The government cannot pick one religion over another. So public policy is based on treating everybody equally under the law. Each religion has the right to decide whom to marry, whom to allow to remarry in that faith, or whom to elevate to priesthood, among other rights.

- Whether being LGBT is a choice or not is irrelevant in this discussion. Religion clearly is a personal choice, and it is (and should be) protected against discrimination. Similarly, sexual orientation and gender identity and expression should be protected, too—even if you believe they are a choice (which they are not).

So what are the areas of the law in which LGBT people are not treated equally?

- Hate crimes
- Nondiscrimination
- Military
- Marriage equality
- Freedom of gender
- Protecting youth
- Same-gender parenting

Each of these areas is an equality goal—what needs to be achieved to be treated equally under the law. Each equality goal is discussed in detail in the successive chapters.

One point to note before we continue: Some people state that the real gay agenda is social justice or to be equal in real life, not just under the law. This is a very honorable objective. However, as we have seen in prior chapters, real equality comes very slowly, even after legal equality is reached. For example, forty-eight years after interracial marriage was made legal in all fifty states by the Supreme Court, some people still oppose it (a significant number of people in some states).

For the real, long-term gay agenda, do not miss reading the epilogue of this book. The immediate focus of our energy is on legal equality under the law. How difficult is this to achieve?

25.

It's Not Rocket Science

"Discrimination is complicated.
Equality is remarkably simple."

—John Lewis,
Legal director of Marriage Equality USA

Some problems are very difficult. Launching a rocket to the moon, landing it there, and bringing the astronauts safely home is a very complex technological challenge. We are the only country in the world to have achieved it. Overhauling the medical system in a country is a difficult problem. Treating everybody equally under the law is not a difficult problem to solve. Here is how it can be done:

1. Examine the areas of the law in which lesbian, gay, bisexual, and transgender individuals are not treated equally. Call these areas equality goals. (This is simple, yet LGBT organizations still talk about issues instead of goals—just check their websites.)

2. Create a way to measure progress at the federal level and in each of the states so you can report accurately how many goals have been achieved.

3. Write these equality goals in legal terms. You can put it all into an omnibus bill. Whether you seek passage as one bill or as a collection of bills is not as critical. An omnibus bill shows, in legal terms, what we need to achieve. It also shows that we are not seeking special rights because the main thing that we are doing is adding the terms *sexual orientation* and *gender identity* in places in current law that protect race, gender, national origin, and religion.

4. Identify the different paths that there are to achieve each goal: By the legislatures, by the courts, and by popular vote.

Different people and different organizations will take different paths to achieve each of the equality goals. Insofar we agree on the goals, different paths are fine because it is very difficult to know in advance which path will lead us to equality faster.

5. Endorse candidates for elected office with clear criteria. Make the endorsement criteria public.

6. Check that endorsed candidates, once elected, sponsor and vote for equality legislation.

7. Legislate to cover *all* the members of the LGBT community.

Understanding what needs to be done is not rocket science. The following chapters examine each of these steps, starting with each of the equality goals to be achieved.

26.

Equality Goal: Nondiscrimination

Mary gets to work to find a note from her boss to see him immediately. Upon entering his office, she can tell that something is wrong.

The boss tells her that she is being fired. She says, "You mean laid off?" The boss says, "No, you are being fired—no layoff package, no unemployment benefits."

Mary is in shock. She thinks about the twelve years she has spent with the company in Florida. In her mind, she goes through the annual raises, the promotions, the wonderful reviews.

She tells the boss, "Tell it to me straight. Why am I getting fired?" The boss doesn't want to tell. Finally, having known Mary for so many years, he talks. The boss says, "My new boss told me that he doesn't want dykes working here."

Mary calls a friend who is an attorney. The attorney says, "I don't need to think about the case very much." Mary is intrigued. The attorney friend continues, "There is absolutely nothing that anyone can do."

Mary is confused. In her state of Florida, like in the majority of states, if the company would have dismissed her by saying that her performance was not good enough, she could have fought it in court by asking them to prove it—given that her annual performance reviews clearly said the contrary. However, because she was dismissed for being a lesbian, there is nothing that she can do. Sexual orientation and gender identity and expression are not protected in her state nor in a majority of states. Nor is it protected by federal legislation.

Protection for sexual orientation also means protection if you are discriminated against for being heterosexual. Say that you are a bartender working in California in a gay bar and you get fired because you are heterosexual (this actually happened). Because

California has a nondiscrimination statute that covers sexual orientation and gender identity and expression, the heterosexual bartender got his job back because you do not need to be gay to be a good bartender in a gay bar.

One of the groups that suffer the most discrimination is people whose gender do not match their gender at birth. Transgender people get severely discriminated against in employment, housing, access to public assistance, and so many aspects vital to everyday life. So it is absolutely critical that, when seeking equality under the law, we always include sexual orientation *and* gender identity.

Fortunately, on April 20, 2012, the EEOC (Equal Employment Opportunity Commission) ruled that transgender and gender non-conforming individuals were covered under Title VII of the Civil Rights Act related to employment nondiscrimination. This ruling is notable, too, because the decision was unanimous, and commissioners were appointed by both Republican and Democratic presidents.

The EEOC ruled in 2015 that gays, lesbians, and bisexuals were also covered under Title VII. This is great progress, but it is limited to employment nondiscrimination and it does not cover other important areas:

- Housing
- Credit
- Public accommodation
- Public facilities
- Federally funded programs and activities

The current strategy is to pass a comprehensive federal Equality Act covering all the areas listed above. This is discussed in more detail in Chapter 57.

Interestingly, most Americans believe that sexual orientation and gender identity and expression are already protected against discrimination in federal legislation and state laws. Here is the reality:

- There is no federal law protecting against discrimination based on sexual orientation or gender identity and expression.

- In the majority of states (twenty-nine states) there is no protection against discrimination based on sexual orientation or gender identity and expression. So, there is some type of nondiscrimination protection in twenty-one states, while LGBT people can marry in thirty-seven states.

Nondiscrimination legislation is a critical battle for equality in our country because it affects so many people. Also, people cannot fight for other rights if they are concerned that they will be fired for being who they are or just for getting married to the person they love. So the battle continues on this front, but we got a sliver of equality in one of the most revered institutions. Read on.

27.

Equality Goal: Marriage Equality

"*Held:* The Fourteenth Amendment requires a
State to license a marriage between two people of
the same sex and to recognize a marriage between
two people of the same sex when their marriage was
lawfully licensed and performed out-of-State."

—US Supreme Court Decision, *Obergefell et al. v.
Hodges*, June 26, 2015

In the historic decision of *Obergefell et al. v. Hodges*, the US
Supreme Court ruled that the US Constitution grants same sex
couples the fundamental right to marry in the same terms as
opposite sex couples, in all fifty states and territories. This is not
only the largest victory for the LGBT rights movement, but for all
people, as the Court explained what it really means liberty and
freedom for all.

In this decision the court addresses the main objections that
opponents of marriage equality presented. It is worth reading the
arguments of the Supreme Court reaffirming equality:

1. **Shouldn't we honor the tradition that marriage is
   between one man and one woman?**

   From the Supreme Court Ruling:

   *The limitation of marriage to opposite-sex couples may
   long have seemed natural and just, but its inconsistency
   with the central meaning of the fundamental right to marry
   is now manifest. [...]*

   *In interpreting the Equal Protection Clause, the Court has
   recognized that new insights and societal understandings*

can reveal unjustified inequality within our most fundamental institutions that once passed unnoticed and unchallenged. [...]

This denial to same-sex couples of the right to marry works a grave and continuing harm. The imposition of this disability on gays and lesbians serves to disrespect and subordinate them. And the Equal Protection Clause, like the Due Process Clause, prohibits this unjustified infringement of the fundamental right to marry.

2. Isn't same sex marriage against the wishes of God?

From the Supreme Court Ruling:

It must be emphasized that religions, and those who adhere to religious doctrines, may continue to advocate with utmost, sincere conviction that, by divine precepts, same-sex marriage should not be condoned. The First Amendment ensures that religious organizations and persons are given proper protection as they seek to teach the principles that are so fulfilling and so central to their lives and faiths, and to their own deep aspirations to continue the family structure they have long revered. The same is true of those who oppose same-sex marriage for other reasons. In turn, those who believe allowing same-sex marriage is proper or indeed essential, whether as a matter of religious conviction or secular belief, may engage those who disagree with their view in an open and searching debate. The Constitution, however, does not permit the State to bar same-sex couples from marriage on the same terms as accorded to couples of the opposite sex.

3. Shouldn't each State have the right to determine who can get married there and deny recognition of marriages performed elsewhere?

From the Supreme Court Ruling:

These cases also present the question whether the Constitution requires States to recognize same sex marriages validly performed out of State. [...]

Being married in one State but having that valid marriage denied in another is one of "the most perplexing and distressing complication[s]" in the law of domestic relations. Williams v. North Carolina, 317 U. S. 287, 299 (1942) (internal quotation marks omitted). Leaving the current state of affairs in place would maintain and promote instability and uncertainty. For some couples, even an ordinary drive into a neighboring State to visit family or friends risks causing severe hardship in the event of a spouse's hospitalization while across state lines. In light of the fact that many States already allow same-sex marriage—and hundreds of thousands of these marriages already have occurred—the disruption caused by the recognition bans is significant and ever growing. [...]

The Court, in this decision, holds same-sex couples may exercise the fundamental right to marry in all States. It follows that the Court also must hold—and it now does hold—that there is no lawful basis for a State to refuse to recognize a lawful same-sex marriage performed in another State on the ground of its same-sex character.

4. Aren't same sex couples disrespecting the institution of marriage, which has always been about the union of one man and one woman?

From the Supreme Court Ruling:

No union is more profound than marriage, for it embodies the highest ideals of love, fidelity, devotion, sacrifice, and family. In forming a marital union, two people become something greater than once they were. As some of the petitioners in these cases demonstrate, marriage embodies a love that may endure even past death. It would misunderstand these men and women to say they disrespect the idea of marriage. Their plea is that they do respect it, respect it so deeply that they seek to find its fulfillment for themselves. Their hope is not to be condemned to live in loneliness, excluded from one of civilization's oldest institutions. They ask for equal dignity in the eyes of the law. The Constitution grants them that right.

5. Wouldn't allowing same sex couples to marry discourage heterosexual couples from marrying?

From the Supreme Court Ruling:

The respondents also argue allowing same-sex couples to wed will harm marriage as an institution by leading to fewer opposite-sex marriages. This may occur, the respondents contend, because licensing same-sex marriage severs the connection between natural procreation and marriage. That argument, however, rests on a counterintuitive view of opposite-sex couple's decision making processes regarding marriage and parenthood. Decisions about whether to marry and raise children are based on many personal, romantic, and practical considerations; and it is unrealistic to conclude that an opposite-sex couple would choose not to marry simply because same-sex couples may do so. See Kitchen v. Herbert, 755 F. 3d 1193, 1223 (CA10 2014) ("[I]t is wholly illogical to believe that state recognition of the love and commitment between same-sex couples will alter the most intimate and personal decisions of opposite-sex couples"). The respondents have not shown a foundation for the conclusion that allowing same-sex marriage will cause the harmful outcomes they describe. Indeed, with respect to this asserted basis for excluding same-sex couples from the right to marry, it is appropriate to observe these cases involve only the rights of two consenting adults whose marriages would pose no risk of harm to themselves or third parties.

6. How does same-sex marriage affect children?

From the Supreme Court Ruling:

Excluding same-sex couples from marriage thus conflicts with a central premise of the right to marry. Without the recognition, stability, and predictability marriage offers, their children suffer the stigma of knowing their families are somehow lesser. They also suffer the significant material costs of being raised by unmarried parents, relegated through no fault of their own to a more difficult and uncertain family life. The marriage laws at issue here thus harm and humiliate the children of same-sex couples.

7. Shouldn't we allow more time to debate the important issue of marriage between two people of the same gender?

From the Supreme Court Ruling:

There may be an initial inclination in these cases to proceed with caution—to await further legislation, litigation, and debate. The respondents warn there has been insufficient democratic discourse before deciding an issue so basic as the definition of marriage. In its ruling on the cases now before this Court, the majority opinion for the Court of Appeals made a cogent argument that it would be appropriate for the respondents' States to await further public discussion and political measures before licensing same-sex marriages. [...]

Yet there has been far more deliberation than this argument acknowledges. There have been referenda, legislative debates, and grassroots campaigns, as well as countless studies, papers, books, and other popular and scholarly writings. There has been extensive litigation in state and federal courts. [...]

As more than 100 amici make clear in their filings, many of the central institutions in American life—state and local governments, the military, large and small businesses, labor unions, religious organizations, law enforcement, civic groups, professional organizations, and universities— have devoted substantial attention to the question. This has led to an enhanced understanding of the issue—an understanding reflected in the arguments now presented for resolution as a matter of constitutional law.

8. Shouldn't same sex marriage be put for a vote or dealt by our elected representatives?

From the Supreme Court Ruling:

Of course, the Constitution contemplates that democracy is the appropriate process for change, so long as that process does not abridge fundamental rights. [...]

An individual can invoke a right to constitutional protection when he or she is harmed, even if the broader public disagrees and even if the legislature refuses to act. The idea of the Constitution "was to withdraw certain subjects from the vicissitudes of political controversy, to place them beyond the reach of majorities and officials and to establish them as legal principles to be applied by the courts." West Virginia Bd. of Ed. v. Barnette, 319 U. S. 624, 638 (1943). This is why "fundamental rights may not be submitted to a vote; they depend on the outcome of no elections."

Having achieved the important equality goal of nondiscrimination in marriage, let's now discuss other equality goals.

28.

Equality Goal: Protecting Youth

One of our obligations in society is to protect our youth, especially in schools, in places of worship, and in homes.

We have to do much better.

What are the effects on LGBT youth when they become homeless because their parents throw them out of the house for being gay, while still underage? What happens when schools are not allowed to teach about sexual orientation or cannot teach about protection to avoid pregnancy and sexually transmitted diseases? What happens when children, and especially LGBT children, are mistreated in the foster care system? What happens when LGBT youth hear the repeated anti-equality messages from so many elected officials? From their teachers? From their parents? What happens when heterosexual children are mistreated just because their parents are LGBT?

Are we a society who cares about our youth or not? Do we provide the safe space in which they can develop to their full potential? Studies show that 85 percent of LGBT students in middle and high school suffered from harassment in the prior school year (check www.GLSEN.org for their pioneering research). Harassment does not provide the safe environment that is needed for youth to study, grow, and develop.

Too many young people have suffered due to wrong-headed beliefs and actions taken by people who are supposed to help our youth like parents, teachers, church leaders, and elected officials. In 2010, all of this came to a head. In July that year, Justin Aaberg, a gay fifteen-year old, died by suicide in Minnesota. In September, it was Tyler Clementi, eighteen, a gay freshman at Rutgers University. Billy Lucas, fifteen and gay, from Indiana, also died by suicide. There was a national outrage, which resulted in a White House summit on bullying.

An important resource to recommend to youth in distress is www.TheTrevorProject.org, which provides crisis intervention and suicide prevention services for LGBT youth.

More than twenty-five years ago, Harvey Milk, the openly gay member of the San Francisco Board of Supervisors who was killed in 1978 by another member of that board, put it best:

> And the young gay people in the Altoona, Pennsylvanias, and the Richmond, Minnesotas, who are coming out and hear Anita Bryant in television and her story. The only thing they have to look forward to is hope. And you have to give them hope. Hope for a better world, hope for a better tomorrow, hope for a better place to come to if the pressures at home are too great. Hope that all will be all right. Without hope, not only gays, but the blacks, the seniors, the handicapped, the us'es, the us'es will give up.

We have not solved the problem yet. LGBT youth continue to suffer tremendously. In September 2010, Dan Savage, a gay columnist, followed a few days later by Joel Burns, a city council member in Fort Worth, Texas, sent a message of hope to teenagers by stating that "It Gets Better." The video by Joel has been watched more than three million times, and the video from Dan and his husband Terry, more than two million times.

As part of the www.ItGetsBetter.org project, many videos have been created and posted online. Here is a startling comparison about political leaders who made an It Gets Better video and whether their counterparts did or not:

- The president of the United States, Barack Obama, found the time to make a video for ItGetsBetter.org.

- The vice president of the United States, Joe Biden, did one, too.

- Democratic presidential contender Hillary Clinton made a video.

- Republican presidential contenders Donald Trump, Ted Cruz, and John Kasich did not.

- Former Democratic Speaker Nancy Pelosi also made a video.

- Republican Speakers John Boehner and Paul Ryan did not.

The list could go on and on. If we cannot take care of *all* of our children, what type of society are we?

Another project of interest is www.Bullyvention.com which aims to use technology to bring together lawmakers and teens. It was started in 2014 by Viraj Puri, who was 13 at the time.

Protecting our youth also means protecting the straight children of LGBT parents. www.COLAGE.org is an organization for young people with lesbian, gay, bisexual, or transgender parents.

The message to our youth is that *it gets better*. It is true that, after the teenage years, things change and do get better but not because the laws are equal. It does get better because you can associate with people who respect you instead of immature middle and high school bullies. Still, however, you will face adult bullies who do not respect the principle that we were all created equal and should be treated equally under the law.

The responsibility of the adults is to *make it better* for bullied youth. We need to pass anti-bullying legislation to end the torment of so many of our young people. We also need to show that we have created a society in which everybody is truly treated the same under the law.

The need for acting against bullying is pressing as it takes a new scale with bullying through the internet ("cyber bullying"), which affects large number of teenagers—gay and non-gay.

In a new development, close to fifty colleges associated with religious institutions are requesting exemption from Title IX of the Civil Rights Act to openly discriminate against students based on their sexual orientation or gender identity.

It is time now to address the next equality goal, also related to children.

29.

Equality Goal: Same-Gender Parenting

"In America, no two families look the same."

—President Barack Obama,
November 1, 2012

Many same-gender couples, like other couples, want to form their own families and have children. This is a fundamental human feeling and a basic right that brings stability to society. For the protection of children, it is very important to have legislation that treats all families equally under the law.

In October 2012, Sophia Bailey Klugh, a ten-year-old, sent a letter to President Obama. It was unprompted by her parents. Here is the letter:
(www.lettersofnote.com/2012/11/our-differences-unite-us.html)

> Dear Barack Obama,
>
> It's Sophia Bailey Klugh your friend who invited you to dinner. You don't remember okay that's fine. But I just wanted to tell you that I am so glad you agree that two men can love each other because I have two dads and they love each other. But at school kids think that it's gross and weird but it really hurts my heart and feelings. So I come to you because you are my hero. If you were me and had two dads that love each other, and kids at school teased you about it, what would you do?
>
> Please respond!

I just wanted to say you really inspire me. I hope you win on being the president. You would totally make the world better place.

Your friend Sophia.

P.S. Please tell your daughters Hi for me!

On November 1, the president responded, while in the mist of his reelection campaign:

Thank you for writing me such a thoughtful letter about your family. Reading it made me proud to be your president and even more hopeful about the future of our nation.

In America, no two families look the same. We celebrate this diversity. And we recognize that whether you have two dads or one mom what matters above all is the love we show one another. You are very fortunate to have two parents who care deeply for you. They are lucky to have such an exceptional daughter in you.

Our differences unite us. You and I are blessed to live in a country where we are born equal no matter what we look like in the outside, where we grow up, or who our parents are. A good rule is to treat others the way you hope they will treat you. Remind your friends at school about this rule if they say something that hurts your feelings.

Thanks again for taking the time to write me. I'm honored to have your support and inspired by your compassion. I'm sorry I couldn't make it to dinner, but I'll be sure to tell Sasha and Malia you say hello.

Sincerely,

Barack Obama

President Obama described the reality of what America is about and our desire to be a diverse, vibrant culture. The question is:

Can same-gender parents be as effective as different-gender parents? Scientific research clearly shows that the answer is yes.

Here is what the American Academy of Pediatrics has to say about it:
(healthychildren.org/English/family-life/family-dynamics/types-of-families/pages/Gay-and-Lesbian-Parents.aspx)

> Studies have shown that children with gay and/or lesbian parents are ultimately just as happy with themselves and their own gender as are their friends with heterosexual parents. Children whose parents are homosexual show no difference in their choice of friends, activities, or interests compared to children whose parents are heterosexual. As adults, their career choices and lifestyles are similar to those of children raised by heterosexual parents.

> Research comparing children raised by homosexual parents to children raised by heterosexual parents has found no developmental differences in intelligence, psychological adjustment, social adjustment, or peer popularity between them. Children raised by homosexual parents can and do have fulfilling relationships with their friends as well as romantic relationships later on.

Here is the conclusion from a report of the American Academy of Pediatrics:
(pediatrics.aappublications.org/content/118/1/349)

> There is ample evidence to show that children raised by same-gender parents fare as well as those raised by heterosexual parents. More than 25 years of research have documented that there is no relationship between parents' sexual orientation and any measure of a child's emotional, psychosocial, and behavioral adjustment. These data have demonstrated no risk to children as a result of growing up in a family with 1 or more gay parents. Conscientious and nurturing adults, whether they are men or women, heterosexual or homosexual, can be excellent parents. The rights,

benefits, and protections of civil marriage can further strengthen these families.

Below, in very clear terms, is the conclusion from the American Psychological Association:
(www.apa.org/helpcenter/sexual-orientation.aspx)

> Social science has shown that the concerns often raised about children of lesbian and gay parents—concerns that are generally grounded in prejudice against and stereotypes about gay people—are unfounded. Overall, the research indicates that the children of lesbian and gay parents do not differ markedly from the children of heterosexual parents in their development, adjustment, or overall well-being.

Professor Judith Stacey of New York University summarizes it very well:
(en.wikipedia.org/wiki/LGBT_parenting)

> Rarely is there as much consensus in any area of social science as in the case of gay parenting, which is why the American Academy of Pediatrics and all of the major professional organizations with expertise in child welfare have issued reports and resolutions in support of gay and lesbian parental rights.

The scientific evidence is clear. Despite this, in 2008, the state of Florida spent $120,000 of taxpayers' money for the testimony of Dr. George Alan Rekers, who was paid to testify in opposition to a lawsuit asking to allow single LGBT people to adopt in Florida—like they can do in *all* other states. Dr. Rekers, a professor and ordained Southern Baptist minister, has written extensively about homosexuality, parenting, and conversion therapy. He also testified on multiple occasions in the past against parenthood by LGBT people, as well as testifying that homosexuality is sinful.

Dr. Rekers has been a major player in denying LGBT people their equality. In the ultimate irony and hypocrisy, it was discovered that in May 2010 Dr. Rekers hired a male prostitute from www.RentBoy.com for a ten-day trip to London and Madrid, with detailed duties for his services. These duties included sexual massages. Frank Rich wrote in the *New York Times* on May 15, 2010:

> Thanks to Rekers's clownish public exposure, we now know that his professional judgments are windows into *his* cracked psyche, not gay people's. But there is nothing funny about the destruction his writings and public activities have sown. His fringe views have not remained on the fringe. His excursions into public policy have had real and damaging consequences on a large swath of Americans.

The suitability of an individual or a couple to be adoptive parents is always reviewed on a case-by-case basis. However, some states discriminate if the individual or couple is lesbian, gay, bisexual, or transgender, without giving them the opportunity to demonstrate that they can be good parents.

We need equal treatment under in the four types of adoption:

1. *Adoption by an individual who is single*

2. *Adoption by a same-gender couple*

3. *Adoption by a member of a same-gender couple of the other's child (called second-parent adoption)*

4. *Adoption as a step parent by a married couple*

The goal of adoption is quickly being fulfilled because of the Supreme Court decision on marriage equality. Still in some states, legislation is being introduced to allow religious adoption agencies to discriminate based on sexual orientation or gender identity of the parents.

Several major LGBT legal organizations have been involved and have been very successful with adoption cases. They are:

- ACLU Lesbian and Gay Rights Project (ACLU.org/LGBT-rights)

- Gay and Lesbian Defenders & Advocates (GLAD.org)

- Lambda Legal (LambdaLegal.org)

- National Center for Lesbian Rights (NCLRights.org)

Along with the work in the states, we need to pass federal legislation—in particular, the Every Child Deserves a Family Act, which does not allow discrimination based on sexual orientation, gender identity, or marital status of the prospective adoptive or foster parent or the sexual orientation or gender identity of the child involved. The standard, in every situation, should be based on the best interests of the child.

Given the scientific evidence and the absolute need for more adoptive and foster parents, it is horrible that some people want to deny children a loving home. Our country is better than that.

A related issue for a parent who is LGBT is to be able to keep custody of his or her child. Custody is customarily decided by the courts in the best interest of the child. One of the most famous cases is the one of Mary Ward, a lesbian who lost custody of her daughter in Florida in 1995 when the judge stated that the daughter should go live with her father, John Ward, to "live in a non-lesbian world."

It did not matter that, by all accounts, the mother was taking great care of the daughter while the father did not express much interest in custody...and the father had been convicted of killing his prior wife. It gets better: He killed her on a rage about custody of their daughter. And then, he sexually abused that daughter. Despite all of this, the judge decided to give custody to him. The documentary about the case is worth watching, *Unfit: Ward vs. Ward.*

Fortunately, things are changing.

Let's discuss the next equality goal.

30.

Equality Goal: Freedom of Gender

"Transgender discrimination is the civil rights issue
of our time."

—Vice President Joe Biden,
October 30, 2012

The majority of people understand the reality that sexual orientation is clearly part of a spectrum ranging from heterosexuality to homosexuality, with bisexuality in between.

However, most people see gender as binary: You are either male or female. The reality is that this is not what happens in nature. While the vast majority of us are either male or female, the Intersex Society of North America defines intersex as "a variety of conditions in which a person is born with a reproductive or sexual anatomy that doesn't seem to fit the typical definitions of female or male" and estimates that "the total of people whose bodies differ from standard male or female is one in 100 births." This is a complex medical issue that goes well beyond having a Y chromosome or not.

You may not have heard of the term "intersex" before and therefore wonder whether this is a new condition. Actually, it has been documented for at least eighteen hundred years; a great example can be found in the Louvre Museum: A Roman sculpture of a beautiful naked female body lying on a marble mattress showing also male genitalia. The sculpture is called the "Hermaphrodite Endormi" ("Sleeping Hermaphrodite").

So not everybody is clearly male or female from a physical perspective. Furthermore, there are people who know that their true gender is not the gender of their birth. As an advanced society, with knowledge based on scientific analysis, we understand the need people have to live their true gender.

Transgender and intersex are different conditions, and organizations fighting for the rights of transgender people and intersex people try to keep them as separate issues. We respect this but note that both intersex and transgender people suffer tremendous discrimination and prejudices from people who are not familiar with the facts.

Similarly, some people are uncomfortable when people do not behave in the expected roles of male or female (this is called gender expression)—maybe a female who is "too butch" or a male who is "too effeminate" or a cross-dresser or a person dressed in a gender-ambivalent manner. Note that gender expression is different from sexual orientation. In any of the examples above, the person might be heterosexual, homosexual, or bisexual.

Many people feel more comfortable with a binary world ("black or white"), but this is not the real world or the world of nature.

Here are some of the hurdles and discriminatory treatment that people face about their gender identity or expression:

- Employment discrimination (fortunately, since 2102 there are legal recourses)

- Lack of healthcare access and insurance coverage

- Inability to declare the appropriate gender in documents (passport, driver's license, Social Security database, and voting ID) to avoid confusion in real life. Several of these issues have been resolved by the Obama administration.

- Access to restrooms

- Air travel scrutiny

- Gender stereotyping

- Military medical and uniform regulations that discriminate against transgender service members

Some people have misgivings about allowing the freedom of gender. Some of these misgivings may be rooted in religious beliefs. Certainly people have the right to hold those beliefs. Other people have the religious belief that God created a complex natural environment, which includes a variety of sexual orientations, gender identities and expressions.

Even very young people can be were aware of their gender identity. Watch this video of a family dealing with a transgender son at age five: www.youtube.com/watch?v=yAHCqnux2fk. This video has been seen almost eight million times.

There is a new generation of people who see gender identity and expression as a spectrum, not necessarily male or female. Like bisexual for sexual orientation, some people identify their sexual identity as bi-gender. This fluidity may be difficult to understand for the majority of people, who were born being comfortable with their biological gender. A good representative of the new thinking is Stephen Ira. He is the twenty-three-year-old son of actors Warren Beatty and Annette Bening. He was born female and transitioned to male at age fourteen and concluded at age seventeen that he was gay. Stephen's video *WeHappyTrans* (www.youtube.com/watch?v=gnZ1pcQIqkQ) has received more than six hundred thousand views on YouTube. In this video, you can clearly see the looks and facial expressions of his father. The press has reported that Stephen has the unconditional love and support of both his parents.

There are some notable organizations working on this goal of freedom of gender: The National Center for Transgender Equality (TransEquality.org), the TransgenderLawCenter.org, and the Woodhull Sexual Freedom Alliance (WoodhullAlliance.org), which takes the perspective of sexual freedom as a fundamental human right.

Most Americans share a common respect for our Constitution and the belief of not letting the government interfere in our most intimate decisions. Because of that, we need to ensure that people with a different gender identity or expression are treated equally under the law and can pursue their personal happiness free from discrimination.

Let's look into the next equality goal in the following chapter—a goal partially achieved.

31.

Equality Goal: Serving in the Military

Finally, on September 20, 2011, the repeal of "Don't Ask, Don't Tell" took effect. This was the legislation passed in 1993 that forced many service members, who are risking their lives for our freedom, to have to live a lie and not have the freedom to be themselves. The support for repeal had become just too big to ignore: 77 percent of Americans supporting repeal (*Washington Post/ABC News* poll, December 15, 2010).

The legislation to repeal "Don't Ask, Don't Tell" was passed in December 2010:

- The House of Representatives voted 250 to 175 for the repeal. Of those voting in favor, 94 percent were Democrats and 6 percent were Republicans. Of those voting against the repeal, 91 percent were Republicans and 9 percent Democrats.

- The Senate voted 65 to 33 for repeal. Of those voting in favor, 88 percent were Democrats or Independents, and 12 percent were Republicans. Of those voting against the repeal, 100 percent were Republican.

However, to gain some Republican support, the legislation was modified at the last moment to eliminate the clause that stated that service members cannot be discriminated against because of their sexual orientation.

It took more than seventeen years to repeal "Don't Ask, Don't Tell." It was a momentous achievement. However, we were let down by a Congress that did only half the job. It took five years since the repeal to add sexual orientation to the nondiscrimination policies of the military. How many more years until we allow transgender members to serve?

Many organizations helped in the repeal of "Don't Ask, Don't Tell," but two of them played a key, long-term role: Servicemembers Legal Defense Network (SLDN.org), which merged with OutServe in 2012, and Palm Center (PalmCenter.org). These organizations are evolving their missions for the new set of needs.

In addition, several individuals led by Lt. Dan Choi and assisted by a new organization, GetEqual.org, added tremendous visibility to the fight not only with the public but also with elected officials, including President Obama and Senate Majority Leader Reid.

It is time to discuss the last equality goal—one that has been achieved at the federal level, but not in most states.

32.

Equality Goal: Hate-Crimes Legislation

This equality goal was achieved at the federal level on October 28, 2009, when President Obama signed into law the Matthew Shepard and James Byrd, Jr. Hate Crimes Prevention Act.

This federal law was named after two well-publicized hate-crime victims who suffered horrifying deaths. James Byrd, Jr., was a heterosexual African-American who was dragged from a pickup truck by three white supremacists in Texas. He was conscious through most of the ordeal, until his head and arm were severed when hitting a curb. The three supremacists continued to drive the truck, dragging the headless body for more than a mile. At that time, in 1998, Texas did not have a hate-crime statute (now it has one, but it does not cover gender identity or expression). The second person for whom the bill is named is Matthew Shepard, a gay student who, also in 1998, was beaten and left to die on a fence in Laramie, Wyoming. At the time, Wyoming did not have any hate-crime statutes either and still does not have one.

Although equality and protection of people would be expected to be a nonpartisan issue, the Matthew Shepard and James Byrd, Jr. Hate Crimes Prevention Act passed Congress in a very partisan manner (like the repeal of "Don't Ask, Don't Tell"):

- In the House of Representatives, the vote was 249 in favor to 175 opposed. Of the votes in favor, 93 percent were cast by Democrats. Of the votes against the legislation, 90 percent were from Republicans.

- In the Senate, the vote was sixty-three to twenty-eight (with nine senators not voting). Of the sixty-three senators voting in favor, 92 percent were Democrats or Independents (Senators Lieberman and Sanders), while all the twenty-eight senators voting against it were Republicans.

The statistics above may appear partisan. The reality is that equality is still a partisan matter in the United States: the majority of Democratic legislators vote in favor of equality while the majority of Republican legislators vote against it.

Equality should not be a partisan matter. Legislators of any party affiliation should agree to what most of the population already agrees with: Every person should be treated equally under the law. A Hart Research poll in 2007 (two years before the legislation was approved) showed that 73 percent of Americans supported hate-crime legislation covering sexual orientation and gender identity and expression. More interestingly:

- Fifty-six percent of Republican men supported hate-crime legislation.

- Sixty-three percent of Evangelical Christians supported it, too.

The definition of sexual orientation covers not only homosexuality, but heterosexuality and bisexuality. So, it is a protection for every person (although note that some people identify as asexual).

While this equality goal has been achieved at the federal level, still much work remains to be done in the states.

There are many misunderstandings about hate-crime legislation:

CLAIM: If a crime is already penalized, there's no need to penalize more because the motivation was hate.

REALITY: Penalties imposed by the judicial system are usually based on motivation and intent. If someone kills somebody by accident, the penalty is less severe than if there was premeditation. Likewise, the penalty should be different when the motivation was hate.

CLAIM: Sexual orientation concerns a special group, and, therefore, sexual orientation does not need to be protected under the law.

REALITY: The law already protects other special groups subject to attack (for example, due to religious beliefs). The law needs to protect sexual-orientation and gender-identity victims because about the same number of them are attacked per year as are those attacked due to their religious beliefs. In addition, sexual orientation covers, by definition, heterosexuals, homosexuals, and bisexuals.

CLAIM: Sexual orientation is a choice (it is not innate), therefore it should not be protected.

REALITY: Science demonstrates that sexual orientation is innate. However, even if it were a choice, it should be protected since religious beliefs (which are clearly a choice) are protected.

CLAIM: Pastors may be tried under this legislation if, after their giving a sermon, a member of the congregation commits a hate crime motivated by the sermon.

REALITY: The hate-crime legislation explicitly includes First Amendment protections toward speech. Hate-crime legislation is about actions and bodily harm against somebody. Freedom of speech is protected: We are always free to think and talk, even hateful speech. Supporters of this legislation included the Presbyterian and Episcopal Churches.

CLAIM: Federal hate-crime legislation means that the federal government will be interfering with local police.

REALITY: The hate-crime legislation has been endorsed by virtually all major law enforcement organizations (including the International Association of Chiefs of Police, the National District Attorneys Association, the National Sheriffs Association, the Police Executive Research Forum, etc.). The police force understands the hideousness of these crimes.

Why is investigating and penalizing hate crimes so important?

The FBI has a clear answer on its website:

> Investigating hate crime is the number one priority of our Civil Rights Program. Why? Not only because hate crime has a devastating impact on families and communities, but also because groups that preach hatred and intolerance plant the seeds of terrorism here in our country.

The most recent FBI statistics indicate that in 2014 there were 1,114 victims of hate crimes in the United States due to sexual orientation or gender identity (down from 1,402 the prior year). This is 10 percent more than the number of victims (1,015) due to religion. It is very important to cover in legislation both types of hate crimes.

Since 1968, there has been a federal hate-crime law that penalizes violent crimes against individuals due to their race, religion, and ethnic origin. However, for forty-one years, there was no federal hate-crime legislation covering such obvious targets as gender, disability, sexual orientation and gender identity until Congress passed this important legislation in 2009.

Let's examine now how we keep score of the progress on all of these equality goals.

33.

Keeping Score

"Success is measured by the civil rights we all
achieve, not by words, access or money raised."

—The Dallas Principles,
Principle #7

It is critical to keep track of progress toward legal equality. To that
effect, eQualityGiving (which this author cofounded) pioneered
two measurements: one at the federal level and one at the state
level.

At the federal level, there are seven major areas of federal law in
which LGBT people are not treated equally. These areas are
addressed by the seven equality goals. Under this measurement,
we have achieved:

- Nondiscrimination in employment has been achieved
  through the Equal Employment Opportunity Commission.
  However, discrimination is still allowed for housing, credit
  and public accommodation—partial goal achieved.

- Marriage equality has been fully achieved.

- Protecting Youth. Not yet achieved.

- Same-gender parenting. Partially achieved because of
  Supreme Court decision on marriage.

- Freedom of Gender. Partially achieved.

- Military: Repeal of "Don't Ask, Don't Tell" has been achieved
  and a nondiscrimination policy for sexual orientation was
  added. However, transgender people still cannot serve
  openly. So, partial goal achieved.

- Hate-crime legislation passed at the federal level—full goal achieved.

Counting achieved goals as one point and partial goals as half a point, the current score is 4 out of 7 (or 57 percent Federal Equality Index).

Much more progress has been made at the state level—although only in a handful of states. For each state, we keep track of six of the seven equality goals (we do not track the goal to serve in the military since most states follow federal law for their national guard). Six states and the District of Columbia have reached a score of 100 percent legal equality for their LGBT residents. Can you guess which states they are?

The six states that have 100 percent equality for LGBT individuals are California, Connecticut, Illinois, Oregon, Vermont, and Washington. Several states are very close: Colorado, Delaware, Iowa, Massachusetts, Nevada, and New Jersey.

Here is an example of why it is important to keep score with uniform measurements: One large state LGBT organization prepared its own analysis of progress in its state and concluded that the state was in the top five states for protecting LGBT individuals from discrimination. The reality is different: The eQualityGiving measure rates their state at 25 percent (which places it toward the bottom). One example of the discrepancy in the results is that the state organization gives itself credit for having a statewide statute protecting against bullying. That statute, however, does not list specific categories of protected youth. Research by GLSEN shows that without enumeration such legislation is not effective at all on protecting individuals.

Do you know where your state stands in LGBT equality?

Take the following quiz:

1. HATE CRIMES: Does your state have hate-crime laws that address violent crimes against individuals due to their sexual orientation *and* gender identity and expression?

   a) Yes
   b) Only sexual orientation is covered in state law

c) No state law (only federal law)
d) Don't know

2. NONDISCRIMINATION: Does your state have laws that forbid discrimination in employment for both private and public employers as well as in housing, finance, and public accommodations due to sexual orientation *and* gender identity and expression?

a) Yes
b) Mostly: sexual orientation and gender identity covered with the exception of public accommodation protection for gender identity
c) Only sexual orientation covered
d) No state law
e) Don't know

3. CIVIL MARRIAGE EQUALITY: Does your state have laws allowing same-gender couples to marry (i.e., get the same civil marriage license as different-gender couples)?

a) Yes
b) Civil unions only
c) Domestic partnerships only
d) No
e) Don't know
(Note, by now we all know the answer to this question, which was the biggest victory for LGBT rights ever.)

4. FREEDOM OF GENDER: Does your state allow a transgender person to obtain a new birth certificate indicating the correct gender?

a) Yes
b) Amended certificate (which shows the prior gender)
c) Decided by court order
d) Depends on city clerk
e) No
f) Don't know

5. PROTECTING YOUTH: Does your state have anti-bullying/anti-harassment laws that specifically list sexual orientation *and* gender identity and expression?

a) Yes
b) Only sexual orientation listed
c) No
d) Don't know

6. SAME-GENDER PARENTING RIGHTS: Does your state allow all qualified LGBT individuals and same-gender couples to jointly adopt, as well as allowing second-parent adoption and step parent adoption?

a) Yes
b) Only single LGBT people can adopt
c) Only single or joint adoption, not second-parent adoption
d) It depends on the jurisdiction—some do allow it
e) Not tested—full extent of parental rights not known
f) No
g) Don't know

You can check the answers for any state and Washington DC here: www.eQualityGiving.org/States-of-Equality-and-Gay-Rights-Scorecard.

In six states and the District of Columbia, the answer to all the questions above is *yes*. However, in the other forty-four states, LGBT people are not treated equally under the law.

34.

What Happened in Dallas?

Two dozen activists, donors, strategists, and former executive directors got together in Dallas on the weekend of May 15–17, 2009, and drafted a unique document called "The Dallas Principles."

The essence of the Dallas Principles is simple:

Full LGBT Equality Now. No Delays. No Excuses.

This may appear like an obvious declaration. It was as obvious then as it is now, and it was as relevant then as it is today. However, in the last seven years, we have heard plenty of excuses to delay equality.

Here is the background: Just after President Obama was first elected in November 2008, as well as during the transition and early months of his presidency, there was interaction between his team and several LGBT organizations. The expectations were high. Everybody understood that there were important priorities to address first (the economy was in shambles, and his policy priority was healthcare). However, it was clear to some of us that many in the LGBT movement were too willing to wait for "the proper time" to achieve equality and that they were buying into the administration's approach to do it incrementally over many years.

eQualityGiving wanted to motivate everybody to push for equality right then, when the conditions were more favorable than they had been in decades, with pro-equality Democrats controlling the White House, the House, and the Senate.

In this spirit, we contacted several people to join us in Dallas. We were careful to select people who were not currently heads of organizations and were mindful of having a balanced representation of gender, sexual orientation, gender identity, and race, as well as different skills and backgrounds. They all accepted, but some had to cancel at the last moment.

Why Dallas? Because it allowed the participants, who came from all over the country, to meet midway (nobody except for the moderator was from Dallas). This would ensure that people wouldn't join just because it was convenient. They really needed to have the commitment to come. Why a couple of dozen people? We wanted to ensure that the meeting was manageable and would create an end product. Everyone had to have a chance to be heard and participate fully.

So, while eQualityGiving convened the Dallas meeting, the Dallas Principles were created as a joint effort of the two dozen authors, everybody participating and everybody sweating the details to have a great product.

What was the impact of the Dallas Principles?

First, it has become very clear that we were right to push for equality immediately. To the dismay of many LGBT organizations, equality did not flow at the speed that they expected in late 2008 and early 2009. We were making progress but not in the timeframe, in the quantity, or at the level that was expected. Then, in 2010, the Democrats lost control of the House as well as many seats in the Senate, and progress come to a standstill (as the Dallas Principles group had predicted).

Second, the Human Rights Campaign started a campaign (which included selling T-shirts) with the slogan "No Excuses" which is part of the Dallas Principles slogan of "Full Equality Now. No Delays. No Excuses."

Third, the Dallas Principles became known well beyond the LGBT community. Vice President Biden was made aware of them, as were key White House staffers, key members of Congress, and members of the Democratic National Committee.

Fourth, the Florida LGBT Democratic Caucus adopted the Dallas Principles as its platform for 2012. After that, for the first time in US history, the platform of a major political party (the Democratic Party) treated LGBT people as fully equal citizens, including the freedom to marry. The Republican Party platform of 2012 is similar to the 2008 platform: An insult to LGBT Americans. Note that the Green Party adopted many years ago a fully pro-LGBT-equality platform.

Fifth, another positive impact of the Dallas Principles is that there is a growing conversation about *full equality NOW*. However, many still say, "I support full LGBT equality now—*but* now is not the time because we do not have a majority in Congress," or any other reason. So, in reality, these people do not believe in full equality now; they believe in *equality later.*

As Dr. Martin Luther King, Jr., said: "A right delayed is a right denied." How quickly we forget.

So, take your sides: are you for *equality now* or *equality later*?

If you are for equality now, you can sign up as an endorser of the Dallas Principles at www.ActOnPrinciples.org/endorsers.

The text of the Dallas Principles and information on its authors appear in Appendix 2.

Let's examine next what is needed to have an inclusive movement for equality.

35.

A Movement for All

"We will not leave any part of our community
behind."

—The Dallas Principles,
Principle #2

For a movement that asks for legal equality for everybody, it is important that we show diversity in all of our efforts. All heads of LGBT organizations believe in diversity. However, much more needs to be done to really show that it is a diverse movement.

GENDER IDENTITY DIVERSITY

In 2007, the movement got a jolt when Representative Barney Frank said that he would strip transgender protections from his proposed Employment Nondiscrimination Act (ENDA) to enhance the chances of its quick passage—eight years later, ENDA has not yet passed. At that time, many prominent LGBT people and the Human Rights Campaign sided with Barney Frank. They said, "Why not pass protections for gays, lesbians, and bisexuals now and come back later with additional legislation for transgender people?" Many others said, "We are all in this together. We cannot leave our transgender friends behind." In just a few weeks, more than three hundred LGBT organizations signed up to push for an inclusive ENDA. A year later, Barney Frank reintroduced an inclusive ENDA. Finally, six months later, the Human Rights Campaign supported it.

Since then, the bipartisan Equal Employment Opportunity Commission ruled that sexual orientation and gender identity were covered for employment nondiscrimination by Title VII of the Civil Rights Act.

Most LGBT organizations include transgender people in their programs. However, transgender people are not adequately represented in the governance of organizations in the movement. Eleven national LGBT organizations do not have a single transgender board member:

- Equality Forum

- Family Equality Council

- GroundSpark

- Immigration Equality

- Log Cabin Republicans

- Movement Advancement Project

- National Stonewall Democrats

- Outserve-SLDN

- Services and Advocacy for Gay, Lesbian, Bisexual and Transgender Elders (SAGE)

- The Trevor Project

- Victory Institute

Notably, the Human Rights Campaign, the largest LGBT organization, which has a forty-nine-member board, only has one transgender member.

In 2012 progress was made: Lambda Legal added a transgender board member, Dr. Jillian Weiss, as did OutServe-SLDN, which appointed a transgender executive director, Allyson Robinson, who also served on the board. In 2013, the National Center for Lesbian Rights appointed Gareth Gill to its board and the Victory Fund appointed Matteus Stephens.

While agreeing on the need for a larger number of transgender board members, executive directors and board chairs provide the following justifications for such a lack of representation:

- *It is difficult to find candidates:* This is true; this is why Dr. Beyer's eQualityGiving project includes a list (with bios) of seventeen qualified transgender people who are willing to serve on national boards.

- *It is even more difficult to find candidates who can meet the financial requirements*: This is true, as some of these organizations expect their board members to contribute or fundraise tens of thousands of dollars every year. However, organizations should remember that the primary function of a board is governance, not fundraising (as most like to think). Organizations can always have another board charged with fundraising or waive or reduce fundraising requirements for some board members.

- *They already cover transgender people in their programs:* This is true in most organizations, but it is not a substitute for organizations that claim to represent lesbian, gay, bisexual, and transgender people to have them on their governing boards.

SEXUAL ORIENTATION DIVERSITY

Too many people are still mistrusting those who self-identify as having a bisexual sexual orientation. They think that bisexuals are closeted gays or lesbians. Granted, bisexuals are a minority of the population, and, granted, when they are acting on their opposite gender attraction, they do not suffer the same discrimination as homosexual individuals. Bisexual people are still misunderstood and not represented appropriately in the LGBT movement (including boards of directors).

For the first time in American history, an openly bisexual person has been elected to Congress: Kyrsten Sinema was elected from Arizona in November 2012.

Furthermore, beyond understanding bisexual people, there are many differences that need to be addressed between gays and lesbians in their approach to giving, politics, and social needs. In summary, many LGBT organizations will benefit from more diversity in sexual orientation.

RACIAL DIVERSITY

The importance of racial diversity (including on boards) is well understood among LGBT organizations. Progress is occurring, but it is still slow. The experiences and needs of white, Latino, Asian, African-American, or Native-American LGBT Americans can be different.

POLITICAL DIVERSITY

About 75 percent of LGBT Americans vote for democrats. This is one of the most solid and consistent voting blocks for the Democratic Party. Yet this party did not bring to a vote the Employment Nondiscrimination Act in 2009–10 while the party had the majority in the House and Senate.

It is important to acknowledge that a minority of LGBT people are Republicans. It is critical to ensure that legislators understand that LGBT equality is a nonpartisan issue. The Log Cabin Republicans work with the minority of Republican legislators who support some LGBT rights. Unfortunately, the majority of Republican legislators in Congress are strongly anti-equality. This is evidenced by their party platform, as well as by their votes against federal hate-crime legislation and repeal of "Don't Ask, Don't Tell."

ECONOMIC DIVERSITY

Much progress needs to occur in supporting the needs of LGBT people who are poor, or destitute youth thrown out of the family's home, or people with chronic diseases such as HIV who do not get appropriate medical care.

36.

Summary: Equal under the Law

"Separate is never equal."

—The Dallas Principles,
Principle #3

A main foundation of American society is the belief that everybody should be treated equally under the law. This is same belief that is the essence of the gay agenda: to be treated equally under the law.

Here are the areas in which heterosexual, homosexual, bisexual, and transgender Americans are not yet treated the same under most states' laws and federal law:

- *Nondiscrimination in employment, housing, credit, public accommodation and facilities, and federally funded programs or activities:* not treated equally at the federal level or in the majority of states.

- *A safe environment for all youth to learn without bullying and harassment*: not achieved at the federal level or in most states.

- *Being able to be a parent and raise a family like everybody else:* need federal legislation and additional legislation in most states. Some progress has occurred because of the marriage decision by the Supreme Court.

- *Free to match your biological gender to your true gender:* partially achieved.

- *Serving in the military without lying about who you are:* Achieved for gays, lesbians and bisexuals but not achieved for transgender people.

- *Hate-crimes legislation:* Achieved at the federal level but not available in most states.

What paths can we take to be better and treat everybody equally under the law? The next chapters show the different ways.

Part III:

Different Paths?

37.

Three Main Paths

There are three main paths to reach legal equality:

1. Courts
2. Legislatures
3. Popular vote

These paths to equality are also used to *deny* equality. For example, putting for a vote the rights of others or legislating blatantly for discrimination (see Chapter 58).

There are always excuses to deny rights, like saying that legislation is needed to "save the children" from gays, or stating that marriage has been between one man and one woman for 2,000 years (not true and irrelevant—discrimination is discrimination even if done for centuries) or saying that LGBT people are asking for special rights (which is not true, as discussed in Chapter 20).

When legislators want to limit our rights, they pass legislation that has big exemptions. For instance, the courts in New Jersey granted full marriage equality in 2013. Some democratic legislators in the state tried to pass equal marriage legislation that had exemptions for religiously affiliated organizations (not just churches, who should be able to marry whoever they want).

Another favored technique by opponents of equality is to go to court or to the legislature claiming that their freedom of religion is at stake, so they want to discriminate against others—in effect, *imposing* their religion on others. This technique is not only used against LGBT rights but also against private family issues such as contraception.

When a court does not want to recognize the fundamental right to being equal, it will usually issue a ruling stating that the matter is to be decided by the legislature (knowing that legislatures, elected by majorities, have a hard time passing laws improving the lives of the minorities).

Finally, when the courts grant equality, as required by the Constitution, opponents often label the judges as "activists" and seek to overturn their rulings by popular vote and even recall or impeach the judges.

In the past, in their disdain for some groups, such as African-Americans, opponents of equal rights went much further by going into a civil war and endangering the whole existence of our incipient nation. Many of these citizens who proclaimed to be for law and order would openly disregard court orders, such as for school integration. Or, worse yet, these citizens would take justice into their own hands, sometimes as part of supremacist organizations.

Fortunately, things are better now. We are not waging civil wars to settle our disagreements, but the willingness to keep some rights and protections only for the majority continues.

As a country, we are better than that. In the next chapters, let's review how the courts, the legislatures, and popular vote can be used to bring equality under the law to *all* Americans, which is a goal we should all aspire to independently of our political beliefs.

38.

Path #1: The Courts

In their brilliance, the Founding Fathers established a government system based on three *independent* branches. This independence among the branches is critical, especially for the legal rights of minorities. It is possible, but difficult, for minorities to get equal rights through legislation. This is because legislators, due to being elected by the majority, look first at legislation that affects the majority. They also may feel pressure from the majority to pass laws that marginalize unpopular minorities—such as criminalizing what consenting adults do in the privacy of their bedrooms or legislating against interracial marriage, as they did in the past.

This is why the role of the courts is to be independent and focus on the Constitution and equality for all instead of the wishes of the majority. So, let's review what the courts said in some important rulings for the LGBT community.

One of the such important decisions was *Lawrence v. Texas*, which, in 2003, struck down all the sodomy laws (which also affected heterosexuals). This was important because some people say that they do not oppose gays, just what they do in bed. Who are they to assume, much less judge, what consenting adults do in the privacy of their bedrooms?

Here is what the US Supreme Court had to say in its majority decision in *Lawrence v. Texas*:

> Liberty presumes an autonomy of self that includes freedom of thought, belief, expression, and certain intimate conduct.

> When sexuality finds overt expression in intimate conduct with another person, the conduct can be but one element in a personal bond that is more enduring. The liberty protected by the Constitution allows homosexual persons the right to make this choice.

> When homosexual conduct is made criminal by the law of the State, that declaration in and of itself is an invitation to subject *homosexual persons to discrimination both in the public and in the private spheres.*

In another important judicial decision, in 2004 the Massachusetts Supreme Judicial Court in *Goodridge v. Department of Public Health* acknowledged that there are different points of view regarding same-gender marriage:

> Many people hold deep-seated religious, moral, and ethical convictions that marriage should be limited to the union of one man and one woman, and that homosexual conduct is immoral. Many hold equally strong religious, moral, and ethical convictions that same-sex couples are entitled to be married, and that homosexual persons should be treated no differently than their heterosexual neighbors.

So the courts agreed that there are differences of opinion, but ruled that *the respect for individual autonomy and equality under the law should trump anything else.* This is the key principle that unites us as Americans. In the end, it comes down to individual autonomy and equality under the law. The court continued:

> Marriage is a vital social institution.
>
> A person who enters into an intimate, exclusive union with another of the same sex is arbitrarily deprived of membership in one of our community's most rewarding and cherished institutions. That exclusion is incompatible with the constitutional principles of respect for individual autonomy and equality under law.

Similar concepts where used by the US Supreme Court in the marriage case (see Chapter 17). Still, despite multiple rulings for equality, some people say these ruling are wrong, made by "activist" judges creating laws instead of just interpreting them. The next chapter carefully examines this concern.

39.

Activist Judges

Some people complain about judicial activism, which popularly means that judges "legislate from the bench." These people believe that judges are taking the power from the people's representatives to create new laws and rights where none exist in the Constitution.

Some judges would like the US Constitution to be read literally, as it was written more than two hundred years ago, as if the world had not changed in the last two centuries. For instance, the role of the president as commander-in-chief also applies to the air force, although planes are never mentioned in the Constitution. Also, fortunately, we no longer accept that any human being could be three-fifths of a person.

Most people complaining about activist judges are conservatives. This criticism is usually addressed from the right at judges who have supported the freedom of individuals to marry the person they love. The reality is that studies show that the US Supreme Court, headed by conservative John Roberts, has been the most "activist" in decades, reversing well established precedents including the controversial ruling in *Citizens United v. Federal Election Commission* (January 21, 2010), in which the Supreme Court ruled that Congress could not impose limits to financial contributions from corporations and unions. This was an expansion well beyond what the Constitution says (which is mute about the subject) and well beyond established precedents.

In fact, in *Citizens United*, the Supreme Court went well beyond the outcome the plaintiff was asking. This is extreme activism. Citizens United, represented by Ted Olson (who represented Bush in 2000 and won the presidency for him), only wanted a ruling that said that long movies showed on a pay-per-view channel did not constitute electioneering and should be allowed to be shown before an election. Olson specifically asked the court not to change precedent about campaign finance legislation. Breaking precedent, restraint, and moderation, the Supreme Court completely changed the financing of elections. (Check the article "Money Unlimited" by Jeffrey Toobin in the *New Yorker*, May 21, 2012.)

Some politicians, such as Newt Gingrich, have gone as far as to state that the president should send the police to arrest a judge to compel appearance in front of a congressional committee to justify his or her rulings (on MSNBC's *Face the Nation*, December 18, 2011). Mr. Gingrich's demand is an attack on democracy.

American democracy is based on three *independent* branches of government. The president (executive branch) cannot order anybody to appear in front of Congress (legislative branch). Similarly, Congress cannot compel judges (judicial branch) to reverse their rulings. Certainly, Congress can create new laws that, if they are constitutional, can have the effect of reversing a ruling. What a sad state of affairs it is when a politician makes such an outrageous statement and tries to undermine our democracy so heavily.

As we said before, the brilliance of American democracy is the separation of powers. Legislators, elected by majority, tend to write legislation that represents the interests of the majority that elected them. Sometimes this legislation unnecessarily hurts a minority. This is why we need the judicial branch that, at the federal level, is not subject to elections to ensure that the rights of the minority are protected. We should all agree to support the *key constitutional principle of independence of judges.*

Let's read next about what the US Supreme Court did for LGBT rights over the years.

40.

Supreme History

"There is dignity in the bond between two men or
two women who seek to marry and in their
autonomy to make such profound choices."

—*Obergefell et al. v. Hodges*, 2015

Below is a summary of the history of LGBT rights as viewed by the Supreme Court in its marriage equality decision, *Obergefell et al. v. Hodges* in 2015. It is worth reading in full:

> [C]hanged understandings of marriage are characteristic of a Nation where new dimensions of freedom become apparent to new generations, often through perspectives that begin in pleas or protests and then are considered in the political sphere and the judicial process.
>
> This dynamic can be seen in the Nation's experiences with the rights of gays and lesbians. Until the mid-20th century, same-sex intimacy long had been condemned as immoral by the state itself in most Western nations, a belief often embodied in the criminal law. For this reason, among others, many persons did not deem homosexuals to have dignity in their own distinct identity. A truthful declaration by same-sex couples of what was in their hearts had to remain unspoken. Even when a greater awareness of the humanity and integrity of homosexual persons came in the period after World War II, the argument that gays and lesbians had a just claim to dignity was in conflict with both law and widespread social conventions. Same-sex intimacy remained a crime in many States. Gays and lesbians were prohibited from most government employment, barred from military

service, excluded under immigration laws, targeted by police, and burdened in their rights to associate. See Brief for Organization of American Historians as Amicus Curiae 5–28.

For much of the 20th century, moreover, homosexuality was treated as an illness. When the American Psychiatric Association published the first Diagnostic and Statistical Manual of Mental Disorders in 1952, homosexuality was classified as a mental disorder, a position adhered to until 1973. See Position Statement on Homosexuality and Civil Rights, 1973, in 131 Am. J. Psychiatry 497 (1974). Only in more recent years have psychiatrists and others recognized that sexual orientation is both a normal expression of human sexuality and immutable. See Brief for American Psychological Association et al. as Amici Curiae 7–17.

In the late 20th century, following substantial cultural and political developments, same-sex couples began to lead more open and public lives and to establish families. This development was followed by a quite extensive discussion of the issue in both governmental and private sectors and by a shift in public attitudes toward greater tolerance. As a result, questions about the rights of gays and lesbians soon reached the courts, where the issue could be discussed in the formal discourse of the law.

This Court first gave detailed consideration to the legal status of homosexuals in Bowers v. Hardwick, 478 U. S. 186 (1986). There it upheld the constitutionality of a Georgia law deemed to criminalize certain homosexual acts. Ten years later, in Romer v. Evans, 517 U. S. 620 (1996), the Court invalidated an amendment to Colorado's Constitution that sought to foreclose any branch or political subdivision of the State from protecting persons against discrimination based on sexual orientation. Then, in 2003, the Court overruled Bowers, holding that laws making same-sex intimacy a crime "demea[n] the lives of homosexual persons." Lawrence v. Texas, 539 U. S. 558, 575.

Against this background, the legal question of same-sex marriage arose. In 1993, the Hawaii Supreme Court held Hawaii's law restricting marriage to opposite-sex couples constituted a classification on the basis of sex and was therefore subject to strict scrutiny under the Hawaii Constitution. Baehr v. Lewin, 74 Haw. 530, 852 P. 2d 44. Although this decision did not mandate that same-sex marriage be allowed, some States were concerned by its implications and reaffirmed in their laws that marriage is defined as a union between opposite-sex partners. So too in 1996, Congress passed the Defense of Marriage Act (DOMA), 110 Stat. 2419, defining marriage for all federal law purposes as "only a legal union between one man and one woman as husband and wife." 1 U. S. C. §7.

The new and widespread discussion of the subject led other States to a different conclusion. In 2003, the Supreme Judicial Court of Massachusetts held the State's Constitution guaranteed same-sex couples the right to marry. See Goodridge v. Department of Public Health, 440 Mass. 309, 798 N. E. 2d 941 (2003). After that ruling, some additional States granted marriage rights to same-sex couples, either through judicial or legislative processes. These decisions and statutes are cited in Appendix B, infra. Two Terms ago, in United States v. Windsor, 570 U. S. ___ (2013), this Court invalidated DOMA to the extent it barred the Federal Government from treating same-sex marriages as valid even when they were lawful in the State where they were licensed. DOMA, the Court held, impermissibly disparaged those same-sex couples "who wanted to affirm their commitment to one another before their children, their family, their friends, and their community." Id., at ___ (slip op., at 14).

Numerous cases about same-sex marriage have reached the United States Courts of Appeals in recent years. In accordance with the judicial duty to base their decisions on principled reasons and neutral discussions, without scornful or disparaging commentary, courts have written a substantial body of law considering all sides of these issues. That case law helps to explain and formulate the underlying principles this Court now must consider. With the exception of the opinion here under review and one other, see Citizens for Equal Protection v. Bruning, 455 F. 3d 859, 864–868 (CA8 2006), the Courts of Appeals have held that excluding same-sex couples from marriage violates the Constitution. There also have been many thoughtful District Court decisions addressing same-sex marriage—and most of them, too, have concluded same-sex couples must be allowed to marry. In addition the highest courts of many States have contributed to this ongoing dialogue in decisions interpreting their own State Constitutions. These state and federal judicial opinions are cited in Appendix A, infra.

After years of litigation, legislation, referenda, and the discussions that attended these public acts, the States are now divided on the issue of same-sex marriage. See Office of the Atty. Gen. of Maryland, The State of Marriage Equality in America, State-by-State Supp. (2015).

This background led to the Supreme Court's historical decision that the US Constitution requires each state and territory to provide marriage licenses and recognize marriages of same-sex couples on the same terms as opposite sex couples.

The next chapters discuss the role of the legislatures for achieving equality.

41.

Path #2: The Legislatures

"The establishment and guardianship of full civil rights is a non-partisan issue."

—The Dallas Principles,
Principle #5

In order to have legislation enacted that treats minorities equally under the law, we need to:

1. Support the election (and reelection) of legislators who are pro-equality. We need to support these candidates independently of their party affiliations (although most are Democrats) and their sexual orientation (many of our biggest supporters are heterosexual).

2. Follow up after the election to ensure that these legislators introduce and support pro-equality legislation.

3. Persuade other legislators to vote for equality legislation. The more they get to know lesbian, gay, bisexual, and transgender constituents, the more they understand their personal plight, the more they support equality legislation.

The following chapters present practical approaches regarding legislative action.

42.

Endorsing Candidates for Elected Office

For the last presidential election, the Democratic Party adopted a platform in the summer of 2012 that for the first time was fully pro-equality (the Green Party has had such a platform for many years). We can expect that the new 2016 platform will be also fully pro-equality while the Republican platform will, like in prior years, condone discrimination. This radically changes how to endorse candidates.

First, as we said in prior editions of the *Gay Agenda,* there is no reason to support (financially or by volunteering) any candidate, from either party, who is not fully pro-equality.

Second, there is now not much point in endorsing in the primaries because in the Democratic Party all the candidates in a race are likely to be pro-equality. If the Republican Party has a pro-equality candidate, then he or she will probably face a pro-equality democrat in the general election.

Multiple organizations endorse candidates under different criteria. For example, the Victory Fund only endorses candidates who are lesbian, gay, bisexual, or transgender. The presence of LGBT legislators is important in the dialog that ensues with other legislators, beyond equality issues. Furthermore, LGBT legislators can help their colleagues understand the impact of their equality votes and have been effective in passing equality legislation. However, there are heterosexual legislators who have been more supportive on equality issues than their LGBT counterparts.

For Congress, in the short term, what we need to achieve full equality is control of the House and the Senate by the Democratic Party, since the Republican Party is not bringing for a vote pro-equality legislation. (To the credit of the Republican leadership, in the last session of Congress they have not brought the Federal Marriage Amendment up for a vote.)

Another organization, Log Cabin Republicans, supports only Republican candidates, but, contrary to the Victory Fund, they endorse independently of sexual orientation. They endorse candidates who are partly pro-equality, since few republicans are fully pro-equality.

The Human Rights Campaign also issues an endorsement list, although the criteria used are unknown.

eQualityGiving, the organization that my husband and I founded in 2005, endorses candidates who support all the equality goals— regardless of party affiliation or sexual orientation or gender identity. The current focus is on *Critical Equality Races;* these are races which meet the following criteria: (1) one candidate is fully pro-equality while the other is anti-equality, (2) the race is close, and (3) the extra funding can make a difference. As stated before, the best bang for the buck in 2016 is in the general elections, instead of the primaries.

To achieve equality, we need to support pro-equality candidates— but all the money invested does not matter if the votes are not counted accurately. We are still not very good at counting votes, as the next chapter discusses

43.

Counting the Votes

If you are investing heavily in politics, either with your money or your time, you should support legislation at the state and federal levels to ensure the auditability of elections and unobstructed voter registration and voting. The problems of the 2000 election have not been corrected, all the contrary.

In November 2000, Americans learned a very important lesson about the most fundamental right in a democracy: the ability to *accurately* and *verifiably* determine who won the election.

That presidential election illustrated a series of problems:

- Unreliable machines that left punch cards with hanging chads

- Butterfly ballots that confused voters

- Bullies banging on the doors of the recount offices, intimidating and forcing to stop the recount

- The limitations of the electoral college as a way to choose a president

- The fact that the presidential election was not decided by 537 votes in Florida but by just one vote in the Supreme Court

The 2000 presidential election showed that each vote makes a difference. What has happened, then, in the last sixteen years to improve our elections?

In October 2002, by a bipartisan vote, Congress approved the Help America Vote Act (HAVA). This legislation has a very significant flaw: it funded the elimination of punch-card and lever machines while recommending that they be replaced by direct recording electronic (DRE) voting machines that cannot be audited. The good news is that there will be no more hanging chads; the bad news is that, wherever paperless DREs are used, there is no way now to verify the voter's intentions.

In early 2005, the Democratic National Committee established a commission (of which I was appointed a member) to analyze whether there was fraud in Ohio in the presidential election of 2004. I created a solution to one of the biggest problems in any election: how to audit the aggregation of the results from each voting station to form the final count for a district or a state. My proposal got much attention and was codified into legislation introduced by Dr. Rush Holt, a rocket scientist, who was the member of Congress representing the Princeton area and the foremost expert in Congress on election law. Unfortunately, this legislation never made it to the floor for a vote.

Meanwhile, in the last few years, the Republican Party has been very proactive and successful in passing legislation in more than a dozen states to make it more difficult for individuals to register to vote and cast their vote. They claim that the purpose of this type of legislation is to ensure that only citizens vote—but this is a false argument since the number of non-citizens voting is extremely small or zero. The real aim of that legislation is to make it more difficult for certain groups of citizens to vote: seniors, minorities, poor people, and college students. These are groups that tend to vote Democrat.

Good organizations working on voting access and auditability include the following:

- Verified Voting (www.verifiedvoting.org)

- Brennan Center for Justice at New York University Law School (www.brennancenter.org)

- Common Cause Education Fund (www.commoncause.org)

- Election Protection Coalition (www.866ourvote.org)

In 2000, counting the votes became all-important because of an activist Supreme Court, which decided the presidential election by one vote. After 2010, counting the money is all-important thanks to an activist Supreme Court, which changed the role of money in elections by one vote.

44.

Counting the Money

Money has always played a role in politics. However, in 2010, the US Supreme Court elevated the role of money in politics to new heights when it ruled in a five to four decision that corporations and unions can spend unlimited amounts of money on political electioneering communications, including advocating for the election or defeat of candidates (*Citizens United v. Federal Election Commission*). The conservative majority of the Supreme Court also decided that such unlimited expenditures do not constitute "a risk of corruption or the appearance of corruption."

Who are they kidding?

Justice Stevens explained in his dissent:

> At bottom, the Court's opinion is thus a rejection of the common sense of the American people, who have recognized a need to prevent corporations from undermining self government since the founding, and who have fought against the distinctive corrupting potential of corporate electioneering since the days of Theodore Roosevelt.

This was a major activist decision, breaking precedent and not giving due deference to Congress (which had imposed limitations on such expenditures). This is exactly the opposite of the restraint that Chief Justice Roberts claimed during his confirmation hearings.

It gets worse: two months after that decision, the Federal Court of Appeals for the DC circuit ruled on the case of *Speechnow.org v. FEC*. The result of both decisions is the creation a new entity: super PACs, which can raise *unlimited amounts of money* from corporations, unions, other groups, and individuals, and they do *not* need to disclose the identity of the donors. They have some trivial limitations: they cannot coordinate with a campaign and cannot make direct financial contributions to campaigns, but they can pay for their own advertisements, even targeting specific candidates.

Continuing to dismantle any limitations to spending on political campaigns, the US Supreme Court ruled in 2014 in the case of *McCutcheon v. Federal Election Commission* that Congress cannot impose limits to the total amount that an individual can donate to a party and federal candidate committees. The next step for the Supreme Court will be to lift any limits that an individual can donate to a candidate.

The are only two main solutions to limit the influence of big money on our democracy. The first one is to wait for the appointment of more liberal judges. The second one is an amendment to the Constitution, which is very difficult; one of the organizations working on this is FreeSpeechForPeople.org.

45.

They Were Wrong

"Those who attempt to divide our community or to delay and deny action on civil equality, waiting for the right moment to arrive, will be held accountable."

—Preamble to the Dallas Principles

As they had done in prior elections, several LGBT people in prominent positions called again for not taking risks before the 2012 election. The argument was that if President Obama was to come out in favor of marriage equality or even sign a non-discrimination executive order, he could lose some of the swing states and then lose the election.

By now we know that they were wrong. The president did come out strongly in support of marriage equality, won nine of the ten swing states, and won reelection. Furthermore, all four states that had marriage equality ballot referenda voted in favor of marriage equality, whereas the issue had lost relentlessly in the past without the President's support.

Why is it still important to highlight this four years later? Not because those political leaders are evil or ill-intentioned. On the contrary, most of them are highly intelligent (some educated in some of the best universities in the world) and well-meaning. They will tell you that they spoke in their personal capacities. However, the press, Congress, and the White House saw them as the leaders of the LGBT movement (even if they may not consider themselves so). What they were saying had impact. So, we need to highlight when they were wrong.

One cannot lead from behind or continue with the same strategies that did not work. The true leaders of the movement are those who are in front, those who propose new ideas, those who think bigger. The following chapters illustrate such a change in approaches.

46.

Insiders and Outsiders

For years, the politics of LGBT equality have been played as an insiders' and outsiders' game—the insiders being open LGBT elected officials, people with positions within the administration or the Democratic Party, or people in certain LGBT organizations (or those who wanted to be in those positions one day); all others were outsiders.

When asked about LGBT equality, insiders would suggest for the most part, small, incremental advances and provide a rationale for why this was not the right time to move forward to fully reach equality, as discussed in the prior chapter. With the release of the Dallas Principles, which asks for full equality now, those insiders would say that they believe in equality, but that it was not the right time.

The outsiders, in the meantime, would criticize the slow progress in achieving equality and would demand more advances right away.

The game would then be played in which astute insiders would point out to the demands of the outsiders and would make requests for more advances (while explaining that they understood the difficult position that the administration or Congress faced).

The first thing that some insiders would do would be to change the demands from the outsiders into requests—most insiders hate the word "demands." The second thing was to provide cover for the decisions made by the administration or Congress since LGBT "leaders" had been consulted. Of course, leadership is not measured by position but by vision and the capability to be in front of (not behind) the needs of those led and to possess the skills to get the job done.

The game needs to change now. It is time for insiders to be in unison with outsiders and demand to achieve full equality now. Without delays. Without excuses.

47.

Politics As the Art of the Possible

"Once you say you are going to settle for second,
that's what happens to you in life."

—President John F. Kennedy

In the last few years, the buzzword sentence among politicians has been: "Politics is the art of the possible." It may sound like a reasonable approach, especially when control of Congress and the presidency is held by different political parties. The problem is who defines what is possible?

Emphasizing what is possible is working in transactional terms in a world that needs transformational actions.

The possible is the art of mediocrity, which is exactly the opposite of what America is all about. We are creators, innovators, frontier-seekers. President Kennedy did not ask, "Is it possible to put a man on the moon?" It was an impossible dream, but he led us to the moon. President Johnson did not ask, "Is it possible to pass the Civil Rights Act?" Initially he did not have the votes, but he got the bill passed. President Lincoln did not ask, "Is it possible to pass the Thirteenth Amendment?" All his advisors told him it was impossible and the leaders of Congress told him that he did not have the votes. Lincoln did pass the Thirteenth Amendment regardless that the war was about to end (and, with it, his major leverage). More recently, in 2011, Governor Cuomo did not ask, "Is it possible to pass marriage equality with a state senate controlled by the Republican party?" He just did it.

As an AT&T marketing slogan says, "Rethink Possible."

Indeed, if anybody tells you that "politics is the art of the possible," suggest that we find true leaders.

48.

Few Republicans Are In

In prior editions of the *Gay Agenda,* we provided a list and commended the notable Republicans who supported marriage equality. With this equality goal reached thanks to the Supreme Court ruling, there are very few Republicans left who openly support equality for the LGBT community:

- Paul Singer, the hedge fund manager who has a gay son, launched the American Unity PAC, that "is focused exclusively on protecting and promoting candidates for US House and US Senate who support freedom for all Americans, regardless of their sexual orientation."

- Senator Mark Kirk (R-IL), the only Republican cosponsor of the Equality Act in the Senate.

- Congressman Robert Dolt (R-IL), the only Republican cosponsor of the Equality Act in the House.

49.

From Endorsements to Legislation: Act on Principles

"Those who seek our support are expected to commit to these principles."

—The Dallas Principles,
Principle #8

Endorsing candidates who are pro-equality is critical for achieving equality under the law. Therefore, we have to ensure that they win despite unlimited and secret financing and although in most states there is no way to audit the results of the election, because of the use of electronic voting machines with no verifiable paper trails.

If, despite all of these obstacles, a pro-equality candidate wins, it is time to get into action—we need to ensure that pro-equality legislators introduce legislation that will bring full legal equality to all Americans. To do so, there is a powerful internet tool: Act On Principles (www.ActOnPrinciples.org), which lists all the federal pro-equality legislation that has been introduced in Congress and identifies how each member of Congress is expected to vote on it. This tool also allows any interested party to update the vote count with any new information. Furthermore, web masters can insert a widget in their sites that keeps the up-to-the-minute vote count.

All parties in Congress and state legislatures use whip counts, which is asking the members of their party how they plan to vote on a piece of legislation. This helps the party leadership determine what to introduce for a vote. Lobbyists also keep their own private whip counts (covering both parties) to determine candidates who need to be persuaded. Whip counts have always been a very closely guarded secret. This new tool makes whip counts open and transparent—quite a revolution. Now there is a simple way to track legislation. This tool was created and is funded by this author; Donald Hitchcock updates the website.

In the last few chapters, we have talked about achieving legal equality through legislation. What about losing rights by popular vote? Isn't voting the essence of democracy? The next chapter addresses these crucial questions and more.

50.

Path #3: Popular Vote

"Fundamental rights may not be submitted to a
vote; they depend on the outcome of no elections."

—US Supreme Court,
West Virginia Bd. of Ed. v. Barnette, 1943

This is a democracy; let's all vote!

Certainly, voting is a critical part of a democracy. However, should
we vote on fundamental rights? For example, how would you like
it if people had a vote on whether *you* have the right to marry?
what if there was a vote for allowing or denying interracial
marriages?

In 1967, when the Supreme Court decided that interracial
marriage should be legal, 72 percent of Americans were opposed
to it and 48 percent supported criminal penalties for interracial
couples who got married (source: www.religioustolerance.org/
hom_mar14.htm).

In November 2000, there was a vote in Alabama to eliminate from
their statutes the prohibition against interracial marriage. Only 60
percent of voters in Alabama agreed to that removal, despite that
the Supreme Court made it illegal to forbid interracial marriages
for thirty-three years before that vote.

As recently as in March 2011, a poll of Republicans voters in
Mississippi revealed that 46 percent of them believe that you
should not have the right to marry somebody of a different race
(source: www.religioustolerance.org/hom_mar14.htm).

So, was it an activist US Supreme Court that allowed interracial
marriages? In fact, the Constitution is silent about marriage.
When the Constitution was enacted, interracial marriage was

forbidden in most states. Fortunately, the Supreme Court in 1967 saw their job as being *independent*. They understood that even if a very large majority of Americans were opposed to interracial marriage, they could not deny the fundamental right of a person to marry the person they love. Also fortunately, we did not take a vote in 1967 about whether interracial marriage should be legal. Clearly it would have lost. The lesson, of course, is that we *cannot put the rights of a minority to a majority vote.*

We have examined so far the three main paths to win (or lose) equality: The courts, the legislatures, and the popular vote. The next chapter will examine other strategies that apply to each of these three main paths.

51.

Winning Hearts and Minds

Whether you follow the path of the courts, the legislatures, or popular votes, a key component for each of them is to win the hearts and minds of the American people, the judges, and the elected officials.

Organizations like GLAAD (glaad.org) have worked very hard for decades to change hearts and minds through the media, and have been joined by other organizations such as EqualityMatters.org. Popular TV shows and movies have helped Americans understand better that there are lesbian, gay, bisexual, and transgender individuals in all occupations, and that, at the end of the day, we are all the same—we are all human beings with our strengths, weaknesses, needs, and accomplishments,

If you are an LGBT person in the closet, the most effective step that you can take to win hearts and minds is to come out to friends, family, coworkers, and everybody. Increasingly more people are accepting and embracing, but it really depends on many factors. Most of your friends and family may already suspect anyway. Also, ask your non-gay friends and family who accept you, to talk to others about acceptance; it will resonate more coming from a heterosexual.

If you cannot endure coming out of the closet or you believe that you are not gay or lesbian or bisexual despite having sex with somebody of the same gender, at least show respect for LGBT people by not tolerating homophobic jokes, by supporting equality policies in your workplace, and by voting only for pro-equality political candidates.

You can express your support for equality in every day-to-day conversation—even with strangers. You can be an activist tourist and make clear to hotel staff, taxi drivers, shopkeepers, and others that you are LGBT and why you are visiting their town.

Sometimes a video can be very impactful. Don't miss: *Love Has*

No Labels www.youtube.com/watch?v=PnDgZuGIhHs   It has been watched 57 million times since introduced on Valentine's Day 2015.

The most important minds to change are those of the people who can change the minds of many others. For instance, whenever you are in front of an elected official, you can always preface any conversation by saying something as short as, "Please pass LGBT equality legislation now," like a female service member who whispered to President Obama, "Please repeal 'Don't Ask, Don't Tell.'" This is what this author did when invited to the White House in 2009. I told the president, the first lady, the vice president, the second lady, and my senator the importance of full LGBT equality. I also handed a letter to President Obama that said, in its entirety (with the italics and bold as in the original):

May 4, 2009

Dear President Obama,

Thank you for taking a moment to read this letter from a gay American.

I came to this country twenty-nine years ago with a Fulbright fellowship when America was the beacon of freedom. I got a doctorate from Stanford University, reached financial success, and retired at age forty. I became a citizen and lived the American dream.

But now America is no longer the leader in civil rights, as gay couples are not treated equally, like they are in many countries, including my former one, Spain.

Many American politicians are following your lead in a call for civil unions, a separate and unequal institution. You continue to express publicly your personal belief that marriage is between a man and a woman—which is clearly discriminatory and contrary to the practice of many religions, including your own.

When you say that you believe marriage is between a man and a woman, please know that those words feel like <u>a knife going through our hearts</u>. It is hurtful to us every time you say that, and it is harmful to our struggle for equal rights.

It would be helpful if you would instead say something like the following:

"As President, it is my duty to make sure all Americans are treated equally.

Our country is deeply divided on this issue.

Some states allow same-gender marriage, some civil unions and domestic partnerships, and some states forbid it in their state constitutions. ***The federal government needs to recognize and treat equally all marriage licenses issued by a state.***

Marriage is also a religious institution. Since the US Constitution states that 'Congress shall make no law respecting an establishment of religion, or prohibiting the free exercise thereof,' ***rest assured that the federal government will not interfere with religions' right to marry who they want. Some religions perform same-gender marriages, and other religions forbid it."***

I am available to discuss this matter with you or your aides at any time.

Sincerely,

Juan Ahonen-Jover, Ph.D.

Three years and four days after getting this letter, President Obama came out in favor of marriage equality. This letter is just one example of the combined effort of thousands of people who made it possible: we won the hearts and minds not only of the American people but of the president of the United States.

Sometimes it takes hard data to convince people of the value of equality. Fortunately, there are several organizations that provide such information:

- The Gay, Lesbian & Straight Education Network (glsen.org) has been working on research in support of safe schools since 1988.

- The Williams Institute, a part of UCLA School of Law, (williamsinstitute.law.ucla.edu) conducts independent research for LGBT laws and public policy.

- Equality Matters (equalitymatters.org) does fact checking on the media and political figures.

- The Palm Center (palmcenter.org) conducts research on LGBT policy matters.

- The Movement Advancement Project (lgbtmap.org) is an independent think tank focused on speeding LGBT equality.

- What We Know (whatweknow.law.columbia.edu) is part of Columbia Law School. It is a new portal focused on bringing together relevant research to inform discussions on current topics.

- The Human Rights Campaign (hrc.org) has several scorecards.

- The Task Force (thetaskforce.org) also issues research reports on hot topics for LGBT equality.

52.

Equal Rights and Businesses

"IF YOU DON'T LIKE GAY MARRIAGE,
DON'T GET GAY MARRIED."

—Billboard advertisement for Manhattan Mini
Storage

While awaiting federal and state legislation to provide non-discrimination, we need to rely on policies adopted voluntarily by businesses. Since 2002, the Human Rights Campaign has kept a Corporate Equality Index; Appendix 3 lists companies with a rating of 100 percent. This index shows tremendous progress by American corporations: 165 of the top Fortune 500 corporations have a perfect rating of 100 percent in 2015 (up from eighty-eight in 2012), and eleven of the top twenty corporations in America reach the same perfect rating. Still, legislation to protect against nondiscrimination is badly needed since the Fortune 500 employs only a small part of the workforce in the United States.

Businesses have known for long time that diversity in their workforce and nondiscrimination policies are good internal measures to keep employees happy. Over time, more businesses have made their support for equality more public. An important milestone in this process was in 2008 with several companies opposing Proposition 8 that took away marriage equality in California.

Another milestone occurred in July 2014 when President Obama signed an executive order requiring that all federal contractors and the federal government do not discriminate in employment based on sexual orientation or gender identity or expression. It covers almost 20 percent of the working population in the United States.

A good example of a company being pro-active about equality is Google, which in 2012 launched a worldwide campaign called

Legalize Love. It is about full LGBT equality, not just marriage. It focuses on countries with a homophobic culture and countries that punish being LGBT.

Another good example is Marriott, which recently joined a coalition to fight the Defense of Marriage Act. Marriott was founded by a Mormon, and his son, Bill Marriott, also a devout Mormon, is the executive chairman. While Bill Marriott personally believes that marriage is between one man and one woman, and he does not drink alcohol, he recently stated, "Our church is very much opposed to alcohol and we're probably one of the biggest sales engines of liquor in the United States. I don't drink. We serve a lot of liquor." He also stated, "We have all the American values: The values of hard work, the values of integrity, the values of fairness and respect." Indeed, these are the values of America and any good business.

A poignant video called *Find Your Understanding* was created by Expedia, the online travel company. It has been watched more than 2.6 million times before it was taken down. It is a wonderful example of a corporation understanding human nature.

Another good example is the series of ads by Honey Maid celebrating all families. In 2014 they had some backlash. Their response was viewed more than four million times. Check it here: www.youtube.com/watch?v=cBC-pRFt9OM

A well-developed rationale of why it is good for business to accept openly LGBT employees is described in the book *The Glass Closet: Why Coming Out is Good for Business* written by Lord John Browne, who is gay, and is the former CEO of British Petroleum.

Many of the largest American companies filed a brief with the Supreme Court supporting marriage equality and they are playing a key role in support of federal LGBT equality and in convincing states not to pass discriminatory legislation against LGBT people.

In 2015, Exxon/Mobil, the third largest corporation in the world by market capitalization, finally added sexual orientation and gender identity to its nondiscrimination policies. It was the most notable company that did not protect its LGBT employees.

A new issue has surfaced after the *Citizens United* decision by the Supreme Court in 2010: Corporations can donate *unlimited* amounts of money for electioneering, and they can do so *anonymously*. For instance, a corporation may be giving to elect conservative candidates to lower corporate tax rates or reduce regulation of an industry. Given that most fiscally conservative candidates are nowadays also socially conservative, the corporations may be giving to candidates who legislate against equality. A corporation may even have a 100-percent rating in the Corporate Equality Index and may even donate to an LGBT nonprofit—while at the same time support candidates who are anti-equality.

To solve this problem requires external pressure as well as inside advocates (in which OutAndEqual.org and employee LGBT groups play a key role). This represents one of the most important and unresolved issues facing our relationship with corporations. It is also a difficult problem to resolve because corporate giving for electioneering can be impossible to track since it can be done anonymously.

In the 2012 elections, some companies, supported by the *Citizens United* decision, took the unprecedented step of sending their employees "voting guides" or letters from the CEO asking all the employees to support certain candidates. For example, Wynn Resorts, which is the third-largest casino company in the country, sent such a voting guide to its twelve thousand employees asking them to vote for conservative candidates—many of whom are anti-equality. Note, ironically, that Wynn Resorts has a 100-percent rating in the Corporate Equality Index from the Human Rights Campaign.

In 2015, when several states rushed to pass discriminatory legislation after the Supreme Court decision on marriage equality, many companies indicated that they would curtail business in that state. Their actions prompted several governors to veto the legislation or their legislative chambers not to proceed. For example, within days of passage of North Carolina bathroom legislation, more than one hundred and fifty business leaders expressed their dissatisfaction. Unfortunately, this legislation has not been repealed (yet).

53.

Building Alliances

Not to state the obvious, but work to reach equality requires building coalitions. We need to:

- Work with the women's political community since it is a big supporter of the LGBT community. In the four states in which marriage equality was on the ballot in 2012, women supported us more than men. In Maine, it was 61 percent of women in favor versus 47 percent of men. In Washington State, 57 percent of women were in favor versus 49 percent of men. In Maryland, the vote was 55 percent of women versus 48 percent of men. In Minnesota, the tally was 56 percent of women versus 46 percent of men. None of the four ballot initiatives would have passed if only men had voted.

- Demonstrate to the African-American community that the LGBT community truly understands its issues, its cultures, and its religious heritages, and that our organizations are truly diverse.

- Help the immigrant communities that, like LGBT people, want to be full US citizens and not second-class ones.

- Continue supporting the disability community, as they have supported the LGBT community.

- Ensure that governing boards for LGBT organizations include gay and lesbian and bisexual and transgender board members.

- Encourage Republican voters to support equality. In the ballot initiative for marriage in Maryland in 2012, in many Republican precincts, marriage equality won a majority despite that President Obama did not carry the precinct.

- Show businesses that LGBT customers are indeed loyal to companies that support equality.

- Demonstrate every day to employers that LGBT employees perform excellently in their jobs.

Alliances can be unexpected and groundbreaking as when gays and lesbians in London supported striking miners in Wales in 1984 creating a fundraising organization called Lesbians and Gays Support the Miners (LGSM). The historic events are brilliantly described in the 2014 movie, *Pride*.

The next chapter summarizes what we've learned in Part III.

54.

Summary: The Paths to Equality

We have seen that there are three main paths to legal equality:

1. *Courts*
   This is the most cost-effective way. We discussed the real meaning of activist judges and why the current conservative Supreme Court is very much activist.

2. *Legislatures*
   It is key to have a high-quality and transparent process for endorsing candidates and then to follow up after the election to ensure that legislation is introduced, supported, and passed.

3. *Popular Vote*
   Putting the rights of a minority up to a vote of the majority is clearly the easiest way to lose equality instead of achieving it.

In addition, for any of the main paths to equality, we need to continue winning hearts and minds and building alliances.

We also discussed the newest issue in our relationship with businesses: some companies are very good with LGBT employees and customers while, at the same time, helping elect anti-cquality legislators who vote or legislate against our rights.

We have examined formal paths to equality. In the next chapters, we'll explore what path *you* can take to make a difference.

Part IV:

What You Can Do In 2016

55.

All Fronts

This year LGBT rights are under attach from all fronts.

The presidential race is at the forefront of our concerns. On one party, the presidential candidates are 100 percent pro-equality. On the other party, totally against equality: they want to define marriage as between one man and one woman; they want to repeal the executive orders signed by Obama to protect federal employees and contractors; they do not support the Equality Act; and they want to nominate Supreme Court justices like Alito and Scalia, who voted against our equal rights. As the general election approaches, tough, the republican nominee may soften his positions, but still the anti-equality stances are entrenched in the vowels of the party.

If John McCain or Mitt Romney (both are more moderate than the current potential Republican nominees) would have won the presidency, we would have not won the marriage equality case, as they made clear that they would have appointed justices like Antonin Scalia. Therefore, it is critical to have a president who believes in appointing judges similar to the ones appointed by Obama.

Even after the groundbreaking marriage decision, the Supreme Court will still play a key role on LGBT equality on topics such as whether the Civil Rights Act protects sexual orientation and gender identity as part of the existing protections for sex, or whether freedom of religion gives the right to discriminate others. A more conservative Supreme Court may even change the marriage equality decision by ruling that marriage is a matter of the states. This would create havoc in the life of the more than one million people currently in same-gender marriages. Therefore, who is president and the composition of the senate while filling the position vacated by Antonin Scalia and future openings is critical for our community.

The races for Congress are stark: The Democratic party, with a platform that supports full LGBT equality, and the Republican party which not only does not support equality, but wants to roll back our progress.

The state races for governor, state attorney general, and members of the state assemblies and senates, are divided the same way as in Congress, but with the difference that multiple states have been successful in passing legislation promoting discrimination based on the misunderstood concept of freedom of religion or passing totally irrational legislation that would create chaos on the simple task of using a public bathroom.

We are currently under attack in 22 states with more than 100 bills intended to discriminate against our community.

So, we need to fight very hard to win in all of these fronts: presidential race, Congress, state races, and state discriminatory legislation. So, we need to win in multiple ballot boxes as well as in the courts and in public opinion.

We are clearly winning in several areas. First, we continue to win the hearts and minds of Americans and support for marriage equality is very strong. Second, well-known businesses are against discrimination of customers or employees and are openly opposing discriminatory legislation passed recently in several states. Third, we are winning the court cases that are trying to limit the protections offered by the Supreme Court ruling on marriage equality. Fourth, we are establishing a legal platform to cover discrimination for sexual orientation and gender identity as discrimination for sex, which is protected in the Civil Rights Act.

Fortunately, in 2016 we are unlikely to face many ballot initiatives like in years past. So far, there is only one potential such measure in Colorado (to allow discrimination based on the religious beliefs of individuals or businesses).

The next chapters address all the work to be done, starting with ten actions that *you* can take.

56.

Your Turn: Ten Actions *You* Can Take in 2016

"Individual involvement and grassroots action are
paramount to success and must be encouraged."

—The Dallas Principles,
Principle #6

Here are ten actions you can take now to advance LGBT equality.
Choose those that are most appropriate for you.

1. VOTE!

The most important thing you can do this year is vote in the
elections and encourage friends and family sympathetic to
equality to also vote, since turnout is critical. If you or your
friends did not vote in the primaries, verify your voter
registration to avoid surprises on election day.

The results of the presidential election will determine what
judges will be appointed to the Supreme Court: similar to
the ones who voted for marriage equality or similar to the
ones who opposed it and may want to overturn it? Also,
which party controls the Senate is important in approving or
rejecting candidates for the Supreme Court. While Donald
Trump will tone down his past opposition to marriage
equality, he has promised to nominate people like Justice
Scalia to the Supreme Court.

In the elections for Congress what is at stake is passing the
Equality Act, which is critical for protecting LGBT people
against discrimination in employment, housing, credit, and
public accommodations.

At the state level, what is at stake is passing legislation for equality and avoid legislation that discriminates based on religious beliefs or tries to legislate bathroom use. Even if in some states is difficult to change the composition of the senate and assembly due to gerrymandering, electing Democratic governors and attorney generals could provide a way to stop damaging legislation.

2. FIGHT DISCRIMINATION IN THE STATES

In 2015, more than 100 bills were introduced in 22 states aimed at discriminating against LGBT people. Most of them are focused on discrimination claiming religious freedom. Other bills are targeting bathroom use by transgender people (see Chapter 14) or allow business to deny service based on sexual orientation or gender identity or marital status and a few promote "conversation therapy" (which is not based on science and is widely considered not effective but damaging to individuals—see Chapter 11).

Take action by lobbying your legislature, voting for pro-equality candidates, and supporting the organizations fighting for equality in the courts and the political system.

3. CREATE DIALOG ABOUT RELIGION'S ROLE

Part I of this book prepared you for discussions with family, friends, coworkers, and others about the freedom of religion. Remember that most religious leaders do not want politicians *to use religion as an excuse for their legislative actions.*

Pope Francis is leading the way towards more acceptance of LGBT people. If you are Catholic, follow his lead.

These discussions are particularly important in view of the push for introducing discriminatory legislation based on "religious freedom."

4. HELP REACH FULL EQUALITY IN STATES

The good news is that in 2015 we added one more state with full LGBT equality. We are fully equal under the law in six states (Illinois, California, Connecticut, Oregon, Vermont, and Washington) and the District of Columbia.

Even in an election year, we need to focus on converting several states to full equality (see Chapter 60).

Check here to see where your state stands:
www.eQualityGiving.org/States-of-Equality-and-Gay-Rights-Scorecard

5. DEMAND FULL EQUALITY

Finally, in 2015 the Equality Act was introduced in Congress. Although it is very unlikely that the Republican majority will bring it for a vote this year, you should make it a requirement for all candidates that you support that they become co-sponsors of the Equality Act if they are in Congress or that they support it if they are not incumbents. Visit their local offices or ask for their support in open town hall meetings.

See Chapter 57 for more information on the Equality Act.

6. BE OUT. DON'T BE SILENT

An important tool to advance equality that everybody can use is our daily conversations with family, friends, coworkers, and even strangers. Don't be silent about your desire to marry the person you love, or about your sexual orientation, or the discrimination that you or other LGBT people face.

Also mention that in the majority of states, you are not protected against discrimination. And, don't be silent when a young person is bullied or a crude joke is told from person to person without anybody complaining.

7. DO MAKE IT BETTER FOR OUR YOUTH

After the far-reaching "It Gets Better" campaign by Dan Savage, the issue is how to *make* it better for our youth *now*. This is a topic that needs to be brought up at every town hall meeting for Republicans and Democrats alike.

8. PUSH FOR FULL LGBT REPRESENTATION IN THE GOVERNANCE OF OUR ORGANIZATIONS

The boards of directors that govern the LGBT organizations need to fully represent the diversity of our movement. Work with the boards and executive directors of the organizations with which you are involved to ensure full representation. There is particular need for more transgender board members. Eleven of our largest national LGBT groups do not have a single transgender board member.

Reread Chapter 35 about what it means to have a movement that is inclusive not just in terms of sexual orientation or gender identity, but in other dimensions as well. Be aware of tokenism.

So, ask any organization that you support with your money or time to have a fully representative governing board.

9. BUILD BRIDGES WITH CORPORATE AMERICA

One of the new challenges after the *Citizens United* decision is that a corporation may give a grant to your favorite LGBT organization while at the same time secretly donating to elect legislators who do not support our equal rights. We need legislation requiring disclosure of corporate donations.

In the meantime, if you are a shareholder activist, you can propose a shareholder vote on disclosure of all the corporate giving.

At the same time, pay attention and support the business that are fighting discriminatory measures, like the famous 2016 Bathroom law passed in North Carolina.

10. BE A DONOR (SMALL OR LARGE)

If you have never given for equality, consider giving to the organizations mentioned in this book. You can also give using crowd funding, in which many people give small amounts to projects sponsored by organizations, companies, or individuals.

Donors tend to get comfortable with a certain level and way of giving. They should consider being bolder givers and take more risks, and support organizations that think bigger and act differently, as well as new organizations and creative individuals with new ideas. A good website to check out is BolderGiving.org. For information on LGBT giving, check eQualityGiving.org, as well as LGBTFunders.org, and review Chapters 63-66 for ideas.

If you are a donor who has contacts with major foundations, point out to them the five-year $50-million effort by the Ford Foundation to fight for LGBT equality announced in November 2012.

11. BONUS: THINK BIG AND ACT DIFFERENTLY

Here is a bonus action that you can take beyond the other ten listed: Think really big and act differently.

Don't be limited by slogans such as *"Politics is the art of the possible"* that tout mediocrity. Don't stop taking action because it is difficult to pass equality legislation when Congress is controlled by the Republican Party. Demand that organizations and elected officials set up specific timetables to reach all the equality goals. Demand full accountability from organizations you donate to: ask for publication of the specific goals they intend to achieve and an annual report of the progress made on achieving those goals.

57.

Equality Act: Equal Once and for All

"Full civil rights for lesbian, gay, bisexual and
transgender individuals must be enacted now.
Delay and excuses are no longer acceptable."

—The Dallas Principles,
Principle #1

Finally, a comprehensive equality civil rights bill was introduced in
2015. In the Senate, the lead sponsor of the Equality Act is Senator
Jeff Merkley (D-OR), who is a straight, fierce ally. In the House,
the lead sponsor is Representative David Cicilline (D-RI), who is
gay.

In 1974, the first bill to protect against discrimination due to
sexual orientation was introduced by Bella Abzug in the House of
Representatives. Year after year it was getting more cosponsors,
but it never got voted on. Fifteen years later, in 1989, it was
reintroduced, focusing only on employment and limited to sexual
orientation under the strategy that a smaller legislation would
have a higher chance to pass.

Despite this strategy of asking for less, forty-two years after the
first bill was introduced, there is still no federal law against
discrimination in employment due to sexual orientation.

In 2005, eQualityGiving created the equality goals. As we have
seen, this is the simple expression in plain English of what is
needed for LGBT people to be equal under the law. Interestingly
enough, the majority (if not all) of the LGBT organizations
structure their websites in terms of *issues* instead of *goals*. This
has an impact on focus, approach, measurements, and what
constitutes success. It has an impact on endorsements for elected

office as well as the expectations about what these candidates should do once they are elected.

In late 2008, eQualityGiving engaged Karen Doering, a well-respected attorney and expert on nondiscrimination legislation, to review federal legislation and prepare a model omnibus legislation to bring equality under the law to LGBT people. The result of her work was the Equality and Religious Freedom Act proposal. It covers thirteen areas of federal law in which we are not yet treated equally:

1. Employment in the private sector
2. Employment in the federal government
3. Housing
4. Public accommodation
5. Public facilities
6. Credit
7. Federally funded programs and activities
8. Education
9. Disability
10. Civil marriage
11. Hate crimes (signed into law in 2009)
12. Armed forces (The "Don't Ask, Don't Tell" Repeal Act was signed into law in 2010)
13. Immigration (which become a moot point with the Supreme Court's Windsor decision in 2013)

This proposal was criticized by some people because it achieved equality by adding the terms "sexual orientation and gender identity" to the Civil Rights Act (CRA). These people claimed that the CRA could not be touched since adding those provisions would open it to add other changes by opponents of the CRA. In reality if the bill had any unwanted changes, it would be vetoed by President Obama.

There was another criticism to our proposal, namely that it would require approval from multiple subcommittees. This is true, but here are the important reasons to introduce a comprehensive bill:

1. *Putting it in writing*

   Since we are seeking legal equality, it is obvious that we need to have a proposed bill with all our goals. This constitutes the gold standard of what is missing to be equal under the law.

2. *No more than others*

The proposed bill demonstrates that LGBT people do not seek "special rights" as the bill basically adds the terms *sexual orientation* and *gender identity* to existing legislation.

3. *No less than others*

This bill is also the standard to compare to partial legislation if approved in smaller pieces. How does a bill compare to the appropriate section of the omnibus bill? Are there any last-minute amendments that compromise our equality? This actually happened in the final negotiations to repeal "Don't Ask, Don't Tell"—important protections were deleted at the last moment.

So, it is wonderful that six years after we presented our proposal the Equality Act has been introduced in Congress doing exactly what we proposed: adding the terms "sexual orientation and gender identity" to the Civil Rights Act.

The Equality Act has 40 co-sponsors in the Senate, all of them Democrats or Independents with the exception of Mark Kirk (R-IL). In the House, it has 174 co-sponsors with Congressman Robert Dolt (R-IL), being the only Republican. This legislation has been endorsed by President Obama.

Furthermore, the Equality Act has received the support of sixty of the largest companies in America, employing more than 4.2 million people.

To pass the Equality Act is currently the top priority for the LGBT movement. This legislation also updates the Civil Rights Act to cover other areas. Check more information in Appendix 4.

58.

The New Frontier: Blatant Discrimination

"Religious beliefs are not a basis upon which to affirm or deny civil rights."

—The Dallas Principles,
Principle #4

The US Supreme Court ruled in June 2014 that a closely-held, for-profit corporation is not required to provide birth control in its insurance coverage based on the sincerely held religious beliefs of its owners.

This decision, *Burwell v. Hobby Lobby,* has broad implications because most of the corporations are closely held (and they can be quite large such as the Koch Industries that employs 100,000 people and had revenues over $115 *billion* in 2014). Even more, this decision opens the gates for these corporations to disregard other laws or regulations that go against their sincerely held beliefs (there is no need to prove that you truly hold these beliefs or that they are part of the dogma of a specific religion). *The bottom line is that this decision allows most employers to impose their religious beliefs onto their employees.*

Going further, legislators across the country introduced starting in 2014 bills that would allow business owners to impose their religious beliefs onto their customers and to discriminate, especially against LGBT people.

There were some victories, like in Arizona and Georgia, when the legislation was vetoed by their governor (Republican in both cases) under pressure from large employers in the state and from many others. Ironically, at the next Georgia GOP convention the governor was censured for vetoing the bill, despite that not doing so would have create significant economic harm to the state.

Before and after US Supreme Court ruling in favor of marriage equality, legislators in several states introduced bills that would put restrictions on judges and court clerks to marry all qualified couples. These legislators have demonstrated a lack of knowledge of the US Constitution and how the separation of powers works.

How far do these bills go? As an example, Oklahoma State Rep. Sally Kern (R), who is well known for her outrageous anti LGBT statements, introduced *three* blatantly discriminatory bills at the same time:

- H.B. 1597, which states: *"No business entity shall be required to provide any services, accommodations, advantages, facilities, goods, or privileges related to any lesbian, gay, bisexual, or transgender person, group or association."*

- H.B. 1598, The Freedom to Obtain Conversion Therapy Act, states: *"The people of this state have the right to seek and obtain counseling or conversion therapy from a mental health provider in order to control or end any unwanted sexual attraction, and no state agency shall infringe upon that right. Parents may obtain such counseling or therapy for their children under eighteen (18) years of age without interference by the state."*

- H.B. 1599, The Preservation of Sovereignty and Marriage Act, states: *"No taxpayer funds or governmental salaries shall be paid for any activity that includes the licensing or support of same-sex marriage. No employee of this state and no employee of any governmental entity shall officially recognize, grant or enforce a same-sex marriage license and continue to receive a salary, pension or any other employee benefit at the expense of taxpayers of this state."* In another section states: *"If a judge violates this act, the judge shall be removed from office..."*

It does not get more unconstitutional than this or more blatantly discriminatory.

59.

The Advocate

President Obama said during the presidential campaign in 2008 that he would be a fierce advocate for LGBT equality. Four years later he came out for marriage equality, and a year later, in his second inaugural address, he said: *"Our journey is not complete until our gay brothers and sisters are treated like anyone else under the law."*

History will show that President Obama was very good for advancing LGBT rights. But we should not forget that a lot of these advances occurred thanks to the constant pressure from donors, activists, organizations, and even Vice-president Biden, with a famous slip that prompted the president to support marriage equality in May 2012. So, like in the famous quote from President Roosevelt ("I agree with you, I want to do it, now make me do it."), we had an ally in President Obama, but we had to Make Him Do It. A good example of that need was the tremendous push the movement had to make for six years to have the president sign the nondiscrimination executive order that he promised in 2008.

For several editions of the *Gay Agenda* we have been pointing out eleven actions that the president could take on his own to expand equality. Here is the status of the actions from last year.

1. NONDISCRIMINATION EXECUTIVE ORDER

Finally, in July 2014, President Obama signed an executive order protecting federal employees and contractors against discrimination based on sexual orientation and gender identity and expression. This was a simple extension of Executive Order 13087, signed by President Clinton in 1998, which protects only federal employees (not federal contractors) and only for sexual orientation (it does not include gender identity or expression). It also extends Executive Order 11246, signed by President Johnson in 1965, which prohibits federal contractors from discriminating based on race, color, religion, sex, or national origin.

This executive order is important in three counts. First, because it covers about twenty-eight million people or about 20 percent of the working population. Second, it does not provide special religious exemptions beyond what is in place already. Third, because now the performance of the contractors regarding nondiscrimination for sexual orientation and gender identity will be part of the regular reviews performed by the Labor Department's Office of Federal Contract Compliance Programs. The department can then initiate investigations based on employees' complaints or third-party complaints and even on its own since often employees are reluctant to file a formal complaint. Furthermore, the department can conduct nondiscrimination trainings at the beginning of a federal contract. This is why this executive order is so important in addition to state and federal legislation.

The Department of Justice is following the rulings by the Equal Employment Opportunity Commission that discrimination in employment due to sexual orientation or gender identity is part of sex discrimination under the Civil Rights Act. This is an important strategy as such cases proceed through federal courts. In addition, we need to pass the Equality Act, which President Obama has endorsed.

2. MARRIAGE EQUALITY

President Obama needs to be commended in this area as indeed he has been vocal on his support for marriage equality since May 2012. Furthermore, his administration has been swift in implementing the 2013 rulings of the Supreme Court, including immediate full equality in benefits for spouses of LGBT service members, social security benefits, full immigration rights, full acceptance by the IRS of same-gender married couples even if they lived in a discriminatory state.

This progress also demonstrated to the Supreme Court and the country, that Americans and the government were ready for the 2015 decision by the Supreme Court that brought marriage equality to all states and territories. The Obama administration has continued reviewing regulations to ensure that the term spouse applies to same-gender couples in existing law such as the Family and Leave Act.

However, as much credit as President Obama deserves, we shall not forget that he is now varnishing his legacy about the delay in accepting marriage equality. He now claims that LGBT friends in long-term relationships helped him understand that civil unions are different from marriage. It is surprising that he did not understand that separate is not equal, despite being a constitutional professor and despite that he indicated he supported marriage equality in a questionnaire in 1996. Ah! politics!

3. OTHER POLICIES

In 2009, President Obama issued a memo to the heads of all the agencies to reduce or eliminate any disparities between same-gender and different-gender couples. This has resulted in a myriad of changes not only for couples but for all LGBT people, especially transgender individuals. The changes took effect on agencies such as the Social Security Administration, the Department of Defense, the Department of Veteran Affairs, the State Department, the Department of Health and Human Services, the Department of Agriculture, and the Department of Housing and Urban Development, among others.

Let's complete the job on this last year of his term!

4. DON'T ASK DON'T TELL

Under the direction of President Obama, his Secretaries of Defense have been strong in implementing equal treatment for all service members. In 2013, nine conservative states refused to provide equal benefits to all married service members in their National Guards; the Secretary of Defense was forceful in requiring all to comply with his directives. All the states complied by the end of that year.

In another success, the 2014 National Defense Authorization Act contained a provision to repeal Article 125 of the military code that forbade full consensual sex (not allowing sodomy) between any couples. This was achieved by the leadership of Senators Kirsten Gillibrand (D-NY) and Mark Udall (D-CO). It was signed into law by President Obama.

in 2015, the Department of Defense added sexual orientation to its Equal Opportunity Policy.

Here are two important items that still need to be completed:

1. Revise the Department of Defense Equal Opportunity Policy to add gender identity (like it has done for sexual orientation); without it, the Department of Defense cannot enforce nondiscrimination.

2. Amend military medical and uniform regulations that discriminate against transgender service members. Allow transgender service members to serve openly. The DoD is actively working on this.

Read the details about what needs to be done at www.eQualityGiving.org/DADT which is maintained by Cap. Tom Carpenter, Esq.

In November 2015, President Obama appointed Eric Fanning as Secretary of the Army but the Senate has yet to act on his nomination despite that he is very qualified. We would become the highest ranking person in the military who is gay.

5. IMMIGRATION EQUALITY

Thanks to the US Supreme Court ruling in *Windsor,* we have achieved equality in immigration for LGBT people. The Obama administration, with the support of LGBT immigration organizations, was very quick in implementing the ruling. For example, in one case a deportation was stopped the same morning that the Supreme Court ruling was issued and, in another case, a gay man obtained his green card two days after the ruling because he was married to an American (the case had been through the administrative process already).

6. TRANSGENDER MEDICAL CARE

Significant progress was made in 2014, when Medicare removed the exclusion for gender-reassignment surgery. This does not mean that surgery and other treatments will be approved by Medicare for each patient, but at least there will not be an automatic exclusion for everybody. Medicaid is more dependent on states' regulations given no federal mandate on this topic.

The exclusion on surgery was also removed from the federal employees' health plans and there is now at least one insurance plan that covers surgery and hormones.

For healthcare plans under the Affordable Care Act ("Obamacare") there is a nondiscrimination policy for gender identity, but this only removes (so far) the exclusion of surgery and does not impose coverage for the procedure. The president needs to push the adoption of nondiscrimination for transgender people in health insurance plans that participate in Obamacare.

In summary, we are making progress but still much more needs to be done on this important issue for transgender people.

7. CABINET MEMBERS

President Obama should appoint an *openly* LGBT cabinet member. This would be an important first in history. Among the many qualified people are Fred Hochberg, currently the chairman and president of the Export-Import Bank and previously the head of the Small Business Administration, and Barney Frank, who was chair for four years of the Financial Services Committee in the House of Representatives.

8. JUDICIAL APPOINTMENTS

When President Obama took office, there was only one openly LGBT federal judge, now there are eleven. This is great progress.

By the end of December 2014, President Obama had appointed, and the Senate had confirmed, 305 federal judges in his years in office. This is in line with the number of appointments by President Clinton and Reagan and about twenty percent more than President George W. Bush at this point of his presidency.

The federal judges appointed by President Obama are much more diverse than in the past. Forty-two percent are women, nineteen percent are African American, eleven percent are Hispanic, and almost four percent are lesbian or gay (unfortunately, none is openly bisexual or transgender).

9. OTHER APPOINTMENTS

President Obama appointed one gay man as ambassador in 2009, five more in 2013 and one more in 2014. He has appointed more openly gay ambassadors than all prior presidents combined. The time has arrived to appoint also lesbian, bisexual, and transgender individuals to such positions.

The president re-appointed in 2013 Professor Chai Feldblum, who is openly lesbian, for another term to the Equal Employment Opportunity Commission, which made the historic ruling in 2012 that transgender individuals are protected against employment discrimination under Title VII of the Civil Rights Act and a similar ruling in 2015 protecting sexual orientation against employment discrimination.

In 2015, the State Department created the new position of Special Envoy for the Human Rights of LGBT Persons and appointed Randy Berry to that position.

Also in 2015, the White House appointed its first transgender staffer, Raffi Freedman-Gurspan. She is outreach and recruitment director for the White House office of presidential personnel.

10. ORGANIZING FOR ACTION

The president has indicated that he will use his campaign group, Organizing for Action (formerly Organizing for America), and its mailing list, to rally Americans in grassroots efforts to pass his legislative agenda.

He should use this list to help pass legislation for LGBT equality, such as the Equality Act. After all, lesbian, gay, bisexual, and transgender people were significant contributors to and volunteers for his campaign.

11. FIERCE ADVOCATE

President Obama promised seven years ago to be a fierce advocate for the LGBT community. Of the eleven actions outlined here last year, he has made great progress on most of them, while two are still pending (Cabinet appointments and Organizing for Action).

Since the president's overall agenda is being stopped by Republicans in the House and Senate, one of his best opportunities for his legacy is to become the president who brought full equality to LGBT Americans. To achieve this depends heavily on the US Supreme Court and Congress, but he can play a very important role by doing all that is possible from the executive branch.

President Obama has clearly indicated that "during his remaining time in office he's going to squeeze every ounce of opportunity that he has out of the presidency."

There is still much to do, as the list above shows. Let's get to work.

60.

Reaching 100 Percent in the States

We can divide the states into three groups.

The first group is the six states (California, Connecticut, Illinois, Oregon, Vermont, and Washington) and the District of Columbia that provide full equality to their LGBT residents according to eQualityGiving's scorecard. Congratulations to all who made it possible!

The second group is the fourteen states that, with a laser focus on full equality, could reach it in the immediate future and join the first group. This group is analyzed in detail in the rest of this chapter.

The third group consists of the thirty other states significantly lagging behind on equality. This group is discussed in the next chapter.

With the Republicans controlling now more state houses than since 1928, gains in equality are more difficult but still possible by taking the momentum generated by marriage equality. How is that you have the right to get married but still can be fired from your job?

Here is what needs to be done in the fourteen states that are the closest to full equality. They are listed by rating and then alphabetical within the same rating:

COLORADO (92%—up from 83% in 2014)

In 2013, Colorado updated the domestic partnerships statute to civil union. In 2014, it got marriage equality, therefore raising its rating.

To go the final mile, Colorado should address any inequalities for transgender people (especially related to amended birth certificates).

DELAWARE (92%—up from 75% in 2014)

Big changes happened in Delaware in 2013 by changing civil unions to full marriage and adding gender identity and expression to the hate crimes and nondiscrimination status. More changes were made in 2014.

Full equality is very close for Delaware: it needs to update its health care provisions for transgender individuals.

IOWA (92%—unchanged since 2012)

This is one of the pioneering states for equality in our country—not just for LGBT rights. Currently, Democrats have a slight majority in the state Senate and are the minority in the House. In 2012, a state Supreme Court justice who voted for marriage equality retained his seat despite a fierce campaign against him.

To reach full LGBT legal equality, Iowa needs to update health care provisions for transgender individuals.

MASSACHUSETTS (92%—up from 83% in 2014)

Massachusetts could have reached 100 percent equality in 2014 when it added protection for transgender people to its anti-bullying statute as well as in housing and employment. However, it did not include protection in public accommodations. The new Republican Governor, Charlie Baker, has indicated that he does not support such protection. In late 2015, the members of Congress representing Massachusetts wrote a letter to the state's house speaker and senate president urging them to pass transgender legislation, which will make the state to reach 100 percent equality.

NEVADA (92%—up from 67% in 2014)

Here is an example of a Republican governor signing two pieces of pro-equality legislation: (1) adding in 2013 gender identity to the state hate crimes statute (which already covered sexual orientation) and (2) creating in 2015 an anti-bullying statute covering sexual orientation and gender identity and expression.

To bring the state to 100 percent need to update health care insurance provisions for transgender individuals.

NEW JERSEY (92%—unchanged since 2012)

New Jersey is very close to reach 100 percent rating. It misses inequalities for transgender people (especially related to amended birth certificates and health care provisions). Legislation for birth certificates passed both the NJ Assembly and Senate, but was vetoed by Republican Governor Chris Christie.

MAINE (83%—up from 75% in 2014)

After the tremendous victory in the popular vote for marriage equality in November 2012, Maine has used the momentum to complete the task for full equality. Only two key items are missing:

1. Add gender identity and expression to the hate-crime statute that already covers sexual orientation.

2. Treat transgender people equally (especially missing is the treatment of birth certificates and health care insurance provisions).

MARYLAND (83%—up from 75% in 2014)

Like Maine, this state passed marriage equality by popular vote in 2012 and has a similar gap to achieve full LGBT legal equality. Here is what needs to be done:

1. Treat transgender people equally (especially missing is the treatment of birth certificates and health care insurance provisions).

2. Ensure, by statute, that LGBT people can become parents by allowing these three types of adoption: single, joint, and second-parent.

MINNESOTA (83%—unchanged since 2014)

After passing marriage equality in 2013, Minnesota needs to complete two items to reach full LGBT equality:

1. Change birth certificates for transgender people as a matter of statute as opposed to the current system, which depends on the courts. Also, add health care insurance provisions for transgender individuals.

2. Ensure, by statute, that LGBT people can become parents by allowing these three types of adoption: single, joint, and second-parent. Also, it is legal to discriminate in the placement of adopted children based on the sexual orientation of the prospective parents.

NEW YORK (83%—unchanged since 2012)

After the bipartisan victory for marriage equality in the state in 2011, New York rates at 83 percent and can reach 100 percent if it achieves a couple of long-sought goals:

1. Add gender identity and expression to the existing nondiscrimination statutes regarding employment, housing, credit, and public accommodations.

2. Add gender identity and expression to the state's hate-crime statute, which already covers sexual orientation.

RHODE ISLAND (83%—up from 58% in 2014)

Rhode Island has a new Democratic governor and an overwhelming Democratic majority in the state senate and house. After passing marriage equality in 2013, here is what needs to be done for full equality:

1. Add gender identity and expression to the hate-crime statute (which already covers sexual orientation).

2. Update health care insurance provisions for transgender individuals.

HAWAII (75%—unchanged since 2014)

After historically passing marriage equality in 2013, two items are still missing:

1. Pass anti-bullying legislation that covers sexual orientation and gender identity and expression.

2. Update health care insurance provisions for transgender individuals.

NEW HAMPSHIRE (75%—up from 67% in 2014)

The heavy lifting has already been done by passing civil unions and later same-gender marriage. This is what is missing:

1. Add gender identity and expression to the hate-crime statute that already includes sexual orientation.

2. Add gender identity and expression to the statutes for non discrimination in employment, housing, credit, and public accommodations (which already include sexual orientation).

3. Ensure that birth certificates indicate the correct gender for transgender people. Add health care insurance provisions to cover transgender individuals.

NEW MEXICO (75%—unchanged since 2014)

The New Mexico Supreme Court ruled in December 2013 in favor of marriage equality. Here is what is missing for full LGBT legal equality:

1. Anti-bullying legislation specifying sexual orientation and gender identity and expression.

2. Add health care insurance provisions to cover transgender individuals.

In 2013, California and the District of Columbia reached full equality. In 2014, it was Oregon and Washington. How many of the fourteen states listed above will reach full LGBT equality in 2016? The time for a big push is now.

What about the other thirty states? Read on.

61.

The Other Thirty States

While six states and the District of Columbia have achieved full LGBT equality and fourteen others could achieve it with a focused push, in the other thirty states it is more challenging. In most of these states, the conservatives control the governorship and the legislature. Progress can be made even in the most conservative thirty states, but opportunities have the be approached state by state.

These thirty states are: Alabama, Alaska, Arizona, Arkansas, Florida, Georgia, Idaho, Indiana, Kansas, Kentucky, Louisiana, Michigan, Mississippi, Missouri, Montana, Nebraska, North Carolina, North Dakota, Ohio, Oklahoma, Pennsylvania, South Carolina, South Dakota, Tennessee, Texas, Utah, Virginia, West Virginia, Wisconsin, and Wyoming.

Here is the status of each equality goal in these states, as a group.

EQUALITY GOAL: NONDISCRIMINATION

This has been an elusive goal to achieve, despite its having been supported for long time by a large majority of Americans and being fundamental for every person's well-being. Without nondiscrimination protections, most people are not able to be out of the closet and be true to who they are and able to contribute to society to their full potential.

Another reality is that, in some more progressive states, the state statutes are stronger than the federal ones. However, conservative states that currently do not have nondiscrimination statutes for sexual orientation and gender identity are not expected to create stronger ones than the proposed federal law.

Of the thirty states in this group, twenty-eight do not offer any nondiscrimination protection for LGBT people. One state,

Wisconsin, offers protection, but limited to sexual orientation. In a great victory in 2015, Utah added nondiscrimination for sexual orientation and gender identity but limited to employment and housing.

Fortunately, through two decisions of the Equal Employment Opportunity Commission, sexual orientation and gender identity are now protected nationwide against employment discrimination under Title VII of the Civil Rights Act—although these rulings do not carry the same weight as federal legislation.

EQUALITY GOAL: MARRIAGE EQUALITY

In 2015, in a historic decision, the US Supreme Court settled the matter of marriage equality in all fifty states and territories.

The decision was implemented without major problems (a couple of hold outs were in Alabama and Kentucky, now resolved thanks to the intervention of LGBT organizations).

EQUALITY GOAL: PROTECTING YOUTH

Of the thirty states in this group, only Arkansas, Alabama, North Carolina and West Virginia offer critical anti-bullying legislation with specific enumeration of sexual orientation and gender identity and expression. Wisconsin offers protection based only on sexual orientation. The other states offer nothing.

Research conducted by GLSEN shows that anti-bullying statutes must identify specific groups protected by the legislation, otherwise it is not effective, so we do not count states with generic policies (such as Florida).

EQUALITY GOAL: PARENTING

Parenting and adoption is mostly a state issue and, in most cases, is handled through the courts on a case-by-case basis rather than by statute. With the advent of same-gender marriage, adoption is becoming more widely available to LGBT couples. Nowadays in all fifty states, a single LGBT person is able to adopt.

EQUALITY GOAL: FREEDOM OF GENDER

There is a multitude of approaches in these thirty states regarding birth certificates:

- In one state (Indiana), there is no indication of gender in the birth certificate.

- In ten states, a new birth certificate is issued with the new gender.

- In three states (Idaho, Ohio, and Tennessee), the original gender in the birth certificate cannot be changed.

- In three states (Montana, Texas, and Wisconsin), a court or court clerk makes the decision.

- In the rest of the states, the birth certificate is amended (still showing the gender at birth).

The model bill regarding changes in birth certificates is the JaParker Deoni Jones Birth Certificate Amendment Act, approved unanimously by the District of Columbia Council in 2013.

Recently, Republican legislators in Florida have introduced a bill to make it very difficult for transgender people to use public restrooms. Similar bills were introduced in Utah and Arizona and failed.

In addition, we need to ensure that health care insurance policies do not exclude treatment for transgender conditions.

EQUALITY GOAL: HATE CRIMES

Since 2009, there has been federal hate crimes legislation which covers sexual orientation and gender identity. This legislation is very useful, but it is not a replacement for hate-crime legislation in the states.

Of the thirty states in this group, only one (Missouri) offers a hate-crime statute covering sexual orientation and gender identity and expression. Nine others offer protection only for sexual orientation. The other twenty offer no protection. There is still a long way to go in many states.

62.

How Much Is Equality Worth to *You?*

Equality doesn't just happen on its own. Many people give substantial amounts of money, time, and talent to make it happen.

The culture of giving is important, regardless of how much money you have. Consider any of the ideas below (or create your own) depending on your financial situation:

1. *Give a few dollars.*
   Most people can donate a few dollars from time to time. No matter how much you can afford, giving helps bring equality.

2. *Give some percentage of your annual income.*
   This is a common formula—for example, give 10 percent of your annual income, as some religious traditions suggest (tithing toward a worthy cause).

3. *Give some percentage of your net assets (or your assets in stock investments).*
   Many experts believe that if you spend less than 4 percent per year of your invested assets, you will not run out of money in your lifctime, and your assets will still keep up with inflation. Of course, this is based on many assumptions, so you need to check with your financial advisor.

4. *Give some percentage of your disposable income.*
   Deduct from your income your basic expenses: Taxes, mortgage, and basic living expenses. Then give some percentage of what's left to advance equality.

5. *Give a part of your annual bonus.*
   In their minds, people do not count bonuses as part of regular income. So why not use part of it to obtain your legal rights (for example, to ensure that you or cannot be fired solely for your sexual orientation of gender identity)?

A SIMPLE GIVING PLAN

There are many causes that deserve your money, but if you or someone you love is lesbian, gay, bisexual, or transgender, why not give first to promote fundamental fairness?

It is easy to create a giving plan. Start by considering three main buckets in which to put your money:

1. Amount you want to give in the next twelve months to advance LGBT equality: $_____

2. Amount you want to give in the next twelve months to other LGBT issues (e.g., HIV, Arts): $_____

3. Amount you want to give in the next twelve months to non-LGBT issues: $_____

For the amount that you want to give to advance equality (first bucket), consider the following split:

- 40 percent for politicians and political organizations that will assist in passing legislation for equality (in election years, maybe this should be 60 percent);

- 40 percent for nonprofits working to achieve equality (in election years, maybe this should be 30 percent);

- 10 percent for opportunity giving (in election years, maybe this is reduced to 5 percent); and

- 10 percent for social-obligations giving (in election years, maybe reduce to 5 percent)

These percentages are just a guideline. Modify them to suit your interests, but it is important to stick to an allocation that makes sense for you and your interests.

A culture of giving will do wonders for your spirit and, combined with the donations of other people, will lead to change.

If you have the financial means, the next chapter is for you.

63.

Strategic and Creative Donors

Advances in equality have occurred because of the dedication and sacrifices of many grassroots volunteers, elected officials, employees of nonprofits, and many donors fortunate enough (and generous enough) to fund the movement.

This chapter focuses on big donors. It discusses fourteen different strategies they can follow for their giving.

There are many terms used to describe strategic philanthropy: intelligent giving, strategic giving, effective philanthropy, venture philanthropy, inspired philanthropy.

Donors, especially mega donors, can create a unique combination of strategies that best fit their needs. They can also decide to withhold funds for strategic purposes. For more details on these strategies, including online resources, please check: www.eQualityGiving.org/Giving-Center.

Here is the summary of fourteen strategies for big donors:

1. IMPACT GIVING

Donors concentrate their giving on a few organizations, political candidates, or equality goals with *large* donations that have a significant impact.

Good for:

- Donors with large budgets
- Donors with solid strategic visions that can change the movement

2. ORGANIZATIONAL GIVING

Donors concentrate most of their giving on a single organization.

Good for:

- Members of the board of that organization, as well as its senior employees
- Donors whose professional interests match the organization direction (e.g., an attorney giving to a legal defense non-profit)

3. GOAL GIVING

Donors concentrate their giving on achieving an equality goal instead of on an organization.

Good for:

- Donors passionate to achieve a specific equality goal (e.g., protecting youth or marriage equality)

4. CONCENTRATED GIVING

Donors give to a limited number of organizations and political candidates.

Good for:

- Donors with more limited budgets
- Donors who are very strategic

5. DISPERSED GIVING

In this strategy, donors give to a multitude of organizations and political candidates.

Good for:

- Donors with large budgets

- Donors who have a hard time saying no
- Donors who fundraise for other causes—this approach creates goodwill among donors who support each other's causes.

6. OPPORTUNITY GIVING

Donors give to take advantage of an immediate opportunity that will achieve a tangible result in a short time (usually a year or less).

Good for:

- Donors who want to see immediate results

7. CAPACITY GIVING

Donors give to build the capacity of an organization or political party and make them more robust over a long time.

Good for:

- Donors who know and trust the senior leadership of the organization and believe in the potential of its mission

8. LOCAL GIVING

Donors give to organizations and politicians in their local communities and states.

Good for:

- Donors who want to make a tangible difference in the lives of their communities
- Donors who want to get to know and influence their local and state politicians

9. MAVERICK GIVING

Donors who want to give to unconventional causes or lesser-known organizations/politicians.

Good for:

- Donors who like to create new paths

10. ANGEL GIVING

Donors who give to help new organizations get established.

Good for:

- Donors interested in social entrepreneurship

11. GAP GIVING

Donors review each of the equality goals and each of the strategic approaches to achieve LGBT equality and give to the areas that are insufficiently funded.

Good for:

- Donors with considerable financial means
- Donors interested in strategic analysis

12. COLLABORATIVE GIVING

Donors give jointly with other donors in the pursuit of a common goal. Examples of this approach are giving circles and some foundations. There are two flavors to collaborative giving: (1) donors give to a fund and a committee distributes the money; or (2) donors are presented with a set of options, and they decide individually how much to give to each of the options.

Good for:

- Donors sharing common passions

- Donors who do not have the time or interest in researching the potential grantees by themselves

13. CONVEYOR GIVING

Donors decide on a goal to be achieved and search for the proper organizations or groups to help achieve it jointly. Donors, in effect, convey a group of organizations and people for a joint goal.

Good for:

- Donors with significant giving capabilities
- Donors respected by the groups that they are conveying
- Donors with the time and abilities to bring together different groups

14. SOCIAL GIVING

Donors give based on social obligations and requests from friends.

Good for:

- Donors who do not want to say no

If you are a big donor, you can use one or more of the strategies presented to maximize the impact of your giving, taking into account your personal situation.

64.

Your Turn: Supporting Organizations

This chapter is for people who are (or want to become) donors to organizations for equality. Before you think about supporting an organization, think about which equality goal you are most passionate about. Is it freedom of gender? Is it employment nondiscrimination? Or another one? Then reread the chapter of this book in Part II that discusses that goal. You will see mentioned there good organizations whose missions are aligned with that goal. Of course, there might be other good organizations (especially at the state level) that may not be mentioned in this book.

Another approach is to focus on the paths to reach equality instead of a specific equality goal. These paths are discussed in Part III of this book. Focusing on a path is very appropriate if you have a specialty that matches it. For instance, if you are an attorney, your focus may not be on a single goal but to reach equality through the courts.

If your focus is religion, check organizations focused on this, such as the InterfaithAlliance.org and the ReligiousInstitute.org. For a different perspective on religion, check FaithInAmerica.org.

When giving to nonprofit organizations, consider these tips:

- *Consider overhead*
  Before giving any significant amount check how much is the overhead compared to total revenue as well as the cost of fundraising compared to total revenue.

- *Give for multiple years*
  Some people recommend three-year commitments, but your commitment should be until a specific goal is reached.

- *Give consistently*
  In election years, it is very tempting to give more for political issues at the expense of the nonprofits. Organizations need stability, so continue supporting them despite the notion that this might be the "election of a lifetime."

- *Check outcomes, not just general progress in the movement*
  What has the organization achieved specifically each year for equality? How relevant is this to achieving legal equality? Does the organization have a written plan with the specific goals to be achieved that year?

- *Help with unplanned opportunities*
  In a perfect world, organizations would know what they are going to do for the whole year. In reality, new funding may be required to take advantage of a new opportunity. For example, an organization may need extra money to fund a survey on a new development. This is not an excuse for organizations that not plan properly. It is helpful to be there for well-managed organizations that want to make the best of a new situation.

- *Ask for goal-based accountability*
  Annual reports that are not based on pre-established goals are of limited value to the board, donors, and volunteers. Ask the organization to announce its goals for the short term and long term and report at least annually on the progress towards those goals. The organization needs to establish clearly what it expects to be its contribution to achieve each specific goal.

- *Ask more*
  The organizations that you support should think big and act differently. They should have a governing board that is fully inclusive of our community, including transgender people.

65.

Acting Differently

"Here's to the crazy ones, the misfits, the rebels, the
troublemakers, the round pegs in the square holes...
because the people who are crazy enough to think
that they can change the world are the ones that
do."

—Original text for the first "Think different"
Apple commercial, 1997
Narrated by Steve Jobs

An important way to accelerate reaching equality is by *acting differently*: Pushing the envelope and creating new ideas and approaches because many times progress comes from unexpected sources. Below are some stories that highlight acting differently. Use them just as pointers. Do not let anyone discourage you from taking action, because nobody really knows which actions will stick and resonate with the public. Go for it!

GOING TO THE SUPREME COURT

The legal organizations working for LGBT equality have done an outstanding job securing more and more victories in the courts, including the critical 2003 victory of *Lawrence v. Texas* in the Supreme Court, which decriminalized homosexuality.

Regarding the right to marry, the LGBT legal organizations have been building the case very carefully and wanted all their ducks in a row before going to the US Supreme Court. All of this changed in 2009 when Chad Griffin, a non-lawyer with significant contacts in Hollywood, asked himself, *Why not bring a marriage case to the Supreme Court now?* Of course, very aware of the risks, he then said, *What if we go to the Supreme Court with a dream team of lawyers?*

There are a couple of attorneys who come up when seeking representation in front of the Supreme Court: Ted Olson, a conservative, who represented George W. Bush in *Bush v. Gore,* the lawsuit in 2000 that decided the campaign for the most important job on the planet; and David Boies, a liberal with extensive Supreme Court experience, who represented Al Gore in the same case. What if you could have a conservative and a liberal, Olson and Boies, both on the same side in front of the Supreme Court, presenting the case for marriage equality? This would be a dream come true! Well, Chad Griffin made it happen (although his approach was considered controversial and risky by many heads of equality organizations). Chad founded the American Foundation for Equal Rights (afer.org) in 2009 and was very successful in raising the funds needed for this lawsuit. Now Chad is the president of the Human Rights Campaign, the largest LGBT political organization.

The Olson-Boies team won marriage equality for California in 2013, although the US Supreme Court did not rule on the constitutionality of same-gender marriage. Two years later, led by another group of lawyers, the Supreme Court ruled that marriage was a fundamental right that applied to same-gender couples nationwide.

GOING BY FOOT

On June 9, 2012, activist Richard Noble completed the first solo walk for LGBT equality across the country, carrying the LGBT flag, and obtaining many proclamations along the way in support of the American Equality Bill—a single, comprehensive bill for LGBT legal equality.

Richard's 2,700-mile walk took fifteen months to complete. Even without receiving much support from most LGBT organizations, the walk achieved its goal of raising awareness for the need for legal equality and doing it now with a single bill. Such a bill, the Equality Act, was finally introduced in Congress in 2015.

GOING TO THE STREETS

November 4, 2008, was a sad day for equal rights: A referendum in California took away the right to marry in that state for same-gender couples. Just two weeks after that vote, there were demonstrations all around the country in support of marriage equality. Who organized these demonstrations? The largest LGBT organizations? No. They were organized by just two people out of Seattle with a computer and much passion and creativity—an example of acting differently and boldly. The right for same-gender couples to marry in California has been restored by the US Supreme Court in 2013.

GOING WILD

A new organization, GetEqual, the brainchild of Paul Yandura and Jonathan Lewis, created quite a bit of good havoc by using civil disobedience techniques. Founded in 2010, it represents the spirit of the Dallas Principles:

Full Equality Now. No Delays. No Excuses.

GetEqual, with its direct actions, such as its members chaining themselves to the fence of the White House, is a key organization to raise awareness that we need equality now. (GetEqual has embraced now a broader mission.)

GOING TO THE WHITE HOUSE

President Obama had promised to repeal "Don't Ask, Don't Tell." Many actions helped to make it happen: the lawsuit won by Log Cabin Republicans, SLDN's lobbying Congress, donors' pushing key senators behind the scenes, a new organization (OutServe) of underground LGBT service members, and many other actions.

An action that was very different was when Dan Choi and several others chained themselves to the White House fence. It had a significant impact on the news and highlighted very publicly the need to repeal "Don't Ask, Don't Tell."

What should have been a small case of civil disobedience became a bigger issue as they got arrested and some of them faced trial (which they won after two years of legal battles).

GOING TO WORK

For forty-two years, we have tried to pass federal legislation to protect against employment discrimination. There have been no results as of yet. So Tico Almeida, an employment attorney who worked as lead counsel in the US House of Representatives on the proposal to ban workplace discrimination against LGBT people, decided to start Freedom to Work in the fall of 2011 focusing on showcasing discrimination. The organization got a great victory in 2015, when it got the Illinois Human Rights Department to rule that Exxon had an anti-gay bias. This is a good example of an organization focusing on a single equality goal to get the job done.

Following an approach similar to the campaign to win marriage, Tim Gill and Paul Singer provided in 2015 the initial funding for the newest LGBT group: Freedom for All Americans, a campaign to win comprehensive nondiscrimination protections both at the federal and state levels by 2020.

GOING TO CHURCH

There are multiple organizations that take the soft approach to work with different religious faiths to make them more accepting of homosexuality. Taking a different approach, Mitchell Gold founded FaithInAmerica.org in December 2005 to directly confront the harm caused by religious bigotry. This is yet another example of a creative individual (he is the cofounder of Gold +Williams furniture design and manufacturing) acting differently. Mitchell Gold wrote an important book about LGBT, *Crisis: 40 Stories Revealing the Personal, Social, and Religious Pain and Trauma of Growing Up Gay in America.*

GOING TO GRADUATE SCHOOL

Chuck Williams noticed an important gap in our tools to achieve LGBT legal equality: The need for rigorous, independent research and scholarship on issues of LGBT law and public policy. So he started the Williams Institute (WilliamsInstitute.law.ucla.edu) in 2001 and hosted it at the UCLA School of Law to demonstrate the seriousness and quality of the research. The Williams Institute has done pioneering research on the census and LGBT demographics, economic impact of marriage equality, parenting, safe schools, and much more.

GOING AFTER THEM

There are several good examples of individuals going after closeted politicians who voted against equality.

For many years, through his www.BlogActive.com website, Mike Rogers reported about politicians that were in the closet while voting against equality. He was instrumental in having several of them to vote in favor of equality.

In 2006, Mark Foley resigned from Congress after Lane Hudson publicized his sexually explicit text messages and emails. This led to an outcry, and many observers credit this case with helping the Democrats to gain back the House of Representatives.

In 2009, Kirby Dick released *Outrage*, a documentary about politicians who are in the closet and vote against equality.

GOING YOUR WAY

The stories above illustrate the importance of creativity and acting differently.

Whether you are a volunteer, a donor, an activist, an ally, the head of an organization, or a bystander, by acting differently, you can achieve what old methods have not. Dream it...and take action.

66.

Your Turn, Your Way

So many equality goals, so many paths to reach equality, so many priorities, so many actions you can take. How do you choose?

Choose your goal based on your *passion*.

Choose your path based on your *skills*.

Moreover, if you have the passion, the skills, and the proper resources for the task (money or time), you can push for equality your own way—without following the established paths.

For example, in September 2010, Dan Savage created, basically single-handedly, the important campaign "It Gets Better." Within two months, President Obama and many others in his administration had produced a video to tell LGBT youth that it gets better.

Here's one more example: A donor friend saw a need in his town to help LGBT high school seniors have their own prom so they could be themselves. He made it happen for fifteen hundred dollars. It has been among the most satisfying cases of giving in his (generous) life as a philanthropist.

Here's a final example: Another friend studied the new restrictive registration laws in Florida and determined ways to comply with them at a minimum cost so that the maximum number of people could be registered. His efforts made a difference in 2012 in this critical battleground state.

So, how do you go about going your own way?

Consider these four approaches:

1. *The Highway*
   In this approach, you go through an established organization (maybe you are on its board or are a volunteer or donor).

Here are the steps that you follow:
1. Have an idea
2. Discuss the idea
3. Present the idea to the board
4. Improve the idea based on feedback
5. Get approval for the idea
6. Fundraise to pay for it
7. Do it!

2. *The Shortcut*
   Here, you just do it yourself—no bureaucracies.
   1. Have an idea
   2. Do it!

   This works very well if you are a very creative person and just use standard (and free) tools such as Facebook, Twitter, YouTube, blogs, and others.

3. *The Expert's Way*
   In this case, you become an expert (for example, in strategic giving) and help make a big step forward for equality. This method requires talent and much patience since it is very time-consuming. But it is priceless.

4. *No Road*
   In the ultimate freedom, you decide not to follow any of the paths above. Just do some constant random acts that move us closer to equality. Be creative. The dots will connect one day.

If you can go on your own path and are very creative, you can have a very significant impact. Remember Apple's commercial quoted at the beginning of Part IV of this book:

> "Here's to the crazy ones, the misfits, the rebels, the troublemakers, the round pegs in the square holes... because the people who are crazy enough to think that they can change the world are the ones that do."

Is this you? It certainly is *me*. The next chapter presents my own path, just as an example.

67.

My Turn, My Way

"A two-man activist factory."

—Jesse Monteagudo

In a review of the 2013 edition of the *Gay Agenda*, Jesse Monteagudo coined the phrase "A two-man activist factory" in referring to the work of my husband and I. Allow me in this chapter to adopt the first person to describe the path I chose. This book is not about theories about equality, it is all based on ideas I have implemented myself.

The path I chose for equality was very simple. First, identify what the goals are (I created the term equality goals). Second, determine the steps required to achieve those goals. Third, create the tools to make this a reality.

In summary, gaining equality under the law is all about creating the intellectual framework of what needs to be done and then creating the tools to do it. In reality, *I am a tool creator*. These tools help accelerate reaching equality.

So here is what this is all about in more detail:

1. IMMEDIATE GOAL: EQUAL UNDER THE LAW

We should not confuse legal equality with social justice or equality in real terms. The immediate and necessary goal is to reach equality under the law.

TOOL CREATED: Equality Goals
By comparing the protections of what other groups have and the LGBT people do not have, it is easy to set the equality goals—the protections under the law that we are missing. These goals are explained in detail in Part II of this book.

TOOL CREATED: eQualityGiving.org website
This website is focused on how donors can accelerate achieving LGBT legal equality. It is organized based on the equality goals. All other major LGBT organizations arrange their websites by issues (which are very different from goals).

2. EQUALITY GOALS IN LEGAL TERMS

Once you have the equality goals, it is important to write them in legal terms so that they can be enacted as legislation.

TOOLS CREATED: Omnibus Equality Bill and American Equality Bill
These tools serve to tell legislators: This is what we want—no more, no less than other groups. This *is* the gay agenda.

These proposed bills also serve as model bills so that, even if legislation is introduced affecting only one part that is covered in the omnibus bill, it serves as a reference in case that bill gets watered down before passage. This legislation was written at my request by Karen M. Doering, Esq., a great lawyer specializing in nondiscrimination law.

The American Equality Bill, championed by J. Todd Fernandez, Esq., is the subset of the omnibus bill that focuses on adding the terms *sexual orientation* and *gender identity* to the Civil Rights Act.

The introduction in Congress in 2015 of the Equality Act, based on the principles mentioned above is an important step for equality. We need to make it law now.

3. STRATEGY TO REACH THE EQUALITY GOALS

Once we have identified the equality goals, it is easy to determine the basic strategy. Which goals are better addressed in states and which ones at the federal level? What's the priority? What's the investment required?

TOOL CREATED: Strategic Matrices
These matrices address the questions above in a clear manner. They are available at

www.eQualityGiving.org/Giving-to-Charity-Guide.

TOOL CREATED: Discussion Network
A network of major and mega donors, executive directors of LGBT organizations, pro-equality elected officials and endorsed candidates, and thought leaders who discuss how to achieve LGBT equality. Actually as disclosed by WikiLeaks, one email from this network was forwarded to then Secretary of State Hillary Clinton by her chief of staff.

4. POLITICAL CANDIDATES ENDORSEMENT AND CRITICAL RACES

Because the main objective is to be equal under the law, endorsing candidates for office is very important—since they are the future legislators who will vote for our equality.

TOOLS CREATED: Endorsement Framework and Endorsed Candidates List
The framework and the endorsement criteria are unique: www.eQualityGiving.org/Endorsements.

This framework is used for actual endorsements in which every candidate submits a questionnaire that can be made public and is personally interviewed (with the exception of President Obama, with whom I spoke but not in a formal endorsement interview):
www.eQualityGiving.org/Endorsed-Candidates

From this information the Critical Equality Races are determined.

5. FOLLOW THROUGH

After the elections, it is very important to follow through and ensure that legislation is being introduced, voted on, and passed.

Is a bill ready to be voted on? How many votes do we have? To answer these questions, the leadership of the House and Senate conduct whip counts, in which they poll members of their own parties about their positions on a piece of legislation. Whip counts are also conducted at the state level. Lobbyists conduct their own whip counts (although usually partially, since it is very labor-intensive).

TOOL CREATED: www.ActOnPrinciples.org
This is a unique tool that makes whip counts public and allows a registered user to update the whip count. There is nothing like it anywhere else. The information is kept up-to-date by Donald Hitchcock.

TOOL CREATED: Platform for Other Contributors
By creating a versatile platform, specific web pages can be created very quickly that allow others to lead important projects. For example:

1. Andrew Tobias, treasurer of the Democratic National Committee, created and keeps updated the most comprehensive list available of accomplishments by the current administration and Congress on LGBT equality:
www.eQualityGiving.org/Accomplishments-by-the-Administration-and-Congress-on-LGBT-Equality.

2. Ret. Captain Tom Carpenter, Esq., created the list of issues pending after the repeal of "Don't Ask, Don't Tell":
www.eQualityGiving.org/DADT.

3. Dr. Dana Beyer lead the project to have more transgender board members so that the governance of our organizations represent the full spectrum of LGBT.

6. MEASURE PROGRESS

Once you have clear goals, it is imperative to measure and report progress.

TOOL CREATED: Federal LGBT Legal Equality Index
It is available here:
www.eQualityGiving.org/Equal-Protection-of-the-Law.

TOOL CREATED: States of Equality Scorecard
This rates every state based on the equality goals; it can be

sorted by state, by score, and by goal. It is available here: www.eQualityGiving.org/States-of-Equality-and-Gay-Rights-Scorecard.

7. THINK BIGGER, ACT DIFFERENTLY—URGENCY

We need a constant sense of urgency to achieve the equality goals. Because too many people are suffering, legal equality is needed right now. To do so, the movement needs to think bigger and act differently.

TOOL CREATED: THE DALLAS PRINCIPLES
I convened the meeting of twenty-four leaders who created the Dallas Principles, which is described in detail in Chapter 34 and Appendix 2 of this book and is also available online: www.TheDallasPrinciples.com.

TOOL CREATED: eQualityThinking
This was a unique conference, described here: www.eQualityThinking.org.

TOOL CREATED: LovingEverywhere.com
A website that asks people to add a picture and sentence about same-gender marriage to emphasize the need for same-gender marriages to be available and be recognized everywhere: www.LovingEverywhere.com.

8. THIS SERIES OF BOOKS

This should be a useful tool since it is intended to be a comprehensive guide to reach legal equality for the LGBT community. Like any good guidebook is updated annually to include the specific actions to take that year.

The final tool mentioned is this book. It includes all my prior work and expands on it—not only the content, but addressing a wider audience. Achieving legal equality is not only important for LGBT people and their allies but for all persons who—independent of their religion or political affiliation—believe in the equality expressed in the United States Constitution and Declaration of Independence.

68.

Summary: All Fronts

This year, being an election year, will determine whether we continue to make progress in equality or stop and even recede.

At immediate stake is to elect a president who continues the path of President Obama and continues to remove administrative impediments to equality as well as be a cheerleader in Congress and the Courts for equality.

It is at stake to continue the international policies of Secretary of State Clinton and Kerry to promote LGBT equality around the world.

There is also the issue of replacing Justice Scalia and possible other vacancies to the Supreme Court.

The elections in the states are also critical to advance equality.

We should continue supporting the LGBT legal and other organizations, as they are fighting legal cases in many states and they provide a cost effective pathway for equality.

Choose your own path to help. You may have time but no cash—then volunteer. You may have cash and no time—then give. Better yet, do both.

Do whatever fits your means, time, personality, passion, and skills. The more you can think bigger and act differently, the better.

This is not the time for delays or excuses. This is not the time for outmoded clichés such as *"politics is the art of the possible."* In reality, *politics is the art of leadership*. This is the time for insiders to publicly push for full equality now (as finally we see them doing). This is the time for the president to be our fiercest public advocate. This is the time for Congress and state legislatures to make true the promise of equality under the law. This is also the time for Republicans to join in the promise of equality written in our Declaration of Independence and our Constitution.

A Respectful Message for *You*

- **To President Obama:** *Thank You! Thank You! This is your opportunity as a fierce advocate in your last year in office.*

  There is one simple goal: LGBT people treated equally under the law. No delays. No excuses.

- **To legislators:** *Equality under the law is what makes the United States of America a great country.*

  Every day that you delay enacting equality legislation, you are affecting real people, and you are not complying with your oath of office.

- **To a religious person:** *Protect your freedom of religion.*

  Your freedom of religion is only possible if others have freedom of religion. This means that we cannot write civil laws based on any particular religion.

- **To parents and grandparents:** *You determine what your family's values are.*

  Do you love all your children equally? Do you treat them equally? Do you want others to do the same?

- **To teenagers:** *Bullying is not cool.*

  Bullies are immature, cruel, and insecure. Definitely not cool.

- **To LGBT teenagers:** *We will make it better.*

  Teenage years are always difficult—more difficult because of the immature bullies. Truly, it gets better. And many people are working hard every day to make it better now.

- **To bullies:** *We know your game.*

  You might be an immature and cruel teenage bully, not understanding the harmful effects that bullying has on somebody's life. Or you might be an adult political bully, intentionally misleading people about what family values are, what freedom of religion entails, or what the Constitution really means and, in doing so, harming the lives of many people. Americans now know your game and will stand up to protect our Constitution, our family values, our individualism, our freedom of religion, and our unalienable right to happiness. *Game over.*

Epilogue: The Ultimate Goal

The gay agenda is simple: To fulfill the American promise to treat every individual equally under the law—independently of their sexual orientation (heterosexual, homosexual, or bisexual) or their gender identity or expression. So it affects every person.

Imagine living in a country in which:

- Each of us is respected and has an opportunity to develop to our maximum capacity.

- Each of us can pursue happiness on our own terms.

- A religion's laws—whether from Bahai, Buddhism, Christianity, Hinduism, Islam, Judaism, Mormonism, or others—are not imposed on nonmembers.

- The courts are truly independent.

- Each of us is judged by our actions and not prejudged because of the color of our skin, our gender, our race, our national origin, our disability, our religion, our sexual orientation, or our gender identity or expression.

This country already exists, and it is bound by a great Constitution and a great maxim inscribed in the façade of the Supreme Court building: Equal Under Law.

What needs to be done is known. Time is of the essence because the current unequal treatment causes real damage to real people. So, let's work for:

Full legal equality now. No delays. No excuses.

As you know from reading this book, full equality under the law is the next step, but what is the ultimate goal?

The ultimate goal is a world without prejudice.

As Mother Theresa said: "If you judge people, you have no time to love them."

The irony is that, on one hand, achieving a world without prejudice is a very difficult goal to reach—almost impossible. On the other hand, it can be reached because each of us has the power to stop prejudging others *right now*.

May we all become inspired and live without prejudice.

Thank *You!*

Countless people engaged daily in achieving equality for the LGBT community have influenced the thoughts expressed in this book and in the eQualityGiving website (where parts of this book appeared first).

These people include the authors of the Dallas Principles; all the members of the Discussion Network of eQualityGiving; the eighty-two panelists and twenty-seven question moderators of eQualityThinking; the webmaster, editors, and champions of Act On Principles; the elected officials eQualityGiving has endorsed over the years; the speakers and participants at OutGiving; and the executive directors and staff of equality organizations who work so hard to achieve equality.

Thanks to Stephen Herbits, Esq., Michael Krawitz, Esq., and David Cockrell who provided many helpful comments over the years.

For more than anybody else, my appreciation and love is for Dr. Ken Ahonen-Jover. He is my soul mate, best friend, sounding board, and husband.

About the Author

Juan Ahonen-Jover, Ph.D., is an entrepreneur who did well and is now doing good. He is an innovator and avid advocate for LGBT rights. He has dedicated the last decade to pursuing the greater good and works diligently with numerous groups and organizations to achieve these ends. He is creator and cofounder of eQualityGiving, ActOnPrinciples, eQualityThinking, Loving Everywhere, and the convener of the Omnibus Bill and the Dallas Principles. He continues to look for new and effective ways to promote the fundamental principle that everyone should be treated equally under the law.

Ahonen-Jover was awarded a Fulbright fellowship and obtained his education in supercomputers and business at Stanford University. He holds four advanced degrees, is fluent in four languages, and is author of a book on computers, as well as multiple titles in his growing *Gay Agenda* series.

To learn more about Ahonen-Jover and/or schedule a speaking engagement, please visit: www.GayAgenda2016.com.

APPENDIX 1:

Notable LGBT People

This appendix lists a few lesbian, gay, bisexual, and transgender people (LGBT) who are particularly notable. The list is not comprehensive, by any means. We cannot understand the gay agenda without knowing some of the LGBT figures and their contributions to society.

How do we know that these people are gay, lesbian, bisexual, or transgender? Some cases are easy since the person publicly announced his or her sexual orientation or gender identity. For others, there is plenty of historical evidence. If you want to learn more about their contributions to society or their coming out status, Wikipedia has good write-ups about them.

POLITICS AND GOVERNMENT

- **Xavier Bettel** (1973–). Gay. Current Prime Minister of Luxembourg since 2013.

- **Elio di Rupo** (1951–). Gay. Prime Minister of Belgium (2011-2014).

- **Johanna Sigurdardottir** (1942–). Lesbian. Prime Minister of Iceland (2009–2013).

- **Per-Kristina Foss** (1950–). Gay. Prime Minister of Norway for a brief period in 2002.

- **Guido Westerwelle** (1961–). Gay. Vice Chancellor of Germany (2009–2011). Foreign Minister of Germany (2009-2013).

- **Pat Carey** (1947–). Gay. Ireland's Minister for Community, Equality and Gaeltacht Affairs (2010–2011).

- **Bertrand Delanoe** (1950–). Gay. Mayor of Paris (2001 - 2014).

- **Klaus Wowereit** (1953–). Gay. Mayor of Berlin (2001 - 2014).

- **Barbara Hendricks** (1952–). Lesbian. German Minister for the Environment (2013–).

- **Jackie Biskupski** (1966–). Lesbian. Mayor of Salt Lake City (2016 -).

- **Ed Murray** (1955–). Gay. Mayor of Seattle (2014 -).

- **Annise Parker** (1956–). Lesbian. Mayor of Houston (2010 - 2016).

- **Christine Quinn** (1966–). Lesbian. Speaker of New York City Council (2006 - 2013).

- **Tammy Baldwin** (1962–). Lesbian. US Senator (2013–) .First female elected from Wisconsin to the US Congress, first openly LGBT person elected to the US House of Representatives (1999–2013), and first openly LGBT person elected to the US Senate.

- **Barney Frank** (1940–). Gay. Former member of the US House of Representatives (1981–2013). Chairman, House Financial Services Committee (2007–2011). First member of Congress to marry a same-gender spouse (2012).

- **Jared Polis** (1975–). Gay. Member of the US House of Representatives (2009–).

- **David Cicilline** (1961–). Gay. Member of the US House of Representatives (2011–).

- **Sean Patrick Maloney** (1966–). Gay. Member of the US House of Representatives (2013–).

- **Mark Pocan** (1964–). Gay. Member of the US House of Representatives (2013–).

- **Mark Takano** (1960–). Gay. Member of the US House of Representatives (2013–).

- **Kyrsten Sinema** (1976–). Bisexual. Member of the US House of Representatives (2003–). First out bisexual elected to Congress.

- **Michael Michaud** (1955–). Gay. Member of the US House of Representatives (2013–2015). Came out as gay in 2013.

- **Gerry Studds** (1937–2011). Gay. First Member of Congress to come out while in office.

- **James McGreevey** (1957–). Gay. Governor of New Jersey (2002–2004).

- **Kate Brown** (1960–). Bisexual. Oregon Secretary of State (2009–2015). First openly bisexual statewide elected official. Became Governor of Oregon (2015–) upon resignation of incumbent.

- **John Berry** (1959–). Gay. US Ambassador to Australia (2013–).

- **James Costos** (1963–). Gay. US Ambassador to Spain (2013–).

- **Rufus Gifford**. Gay. US Ambassador to Denmark (2013–).

- **James "Wally" Brewster** (1960–). Gay. US Ambassador to the Dominican Republic (2013–).

- **Daniel Baer**. Gay. US Ambassador to the Organization for Security and Cooperation in Europe (2013–).

- **Ted Osius**. Gay. US Ambassador to Vietnam (2014–).

- **David Huebner** (1960–). Gay. US Ambassador to New Zealand and Samoa (2009–2014).

- **James Hormel** (1933–). Gay. Philanthropist. First openly LGBT ambassador to the United States (Luxembourg, 1999). Appointed during recess (Senate wouldn't confirm him).

- **Michael Guest** (1957–). Gay. Former US Ambassador to Romania (2001–2004). First openly gay ambassador to be confirmed by Senate. Retired in 2007 in protest for LGBT discrimination in the State Department.

- **Harvey Milk** (1930–1978). Gay. Member of San Francisco Board of Supervisors, who was murdered along with Mayor Moscone by a fellow supervisor.

- **Nancy Wechsler** (1950–). Lesbian. First open LGBT person elected to office in the United States (Ann Arbor City Council, 1972).

- **Angie Buhl** (1985–). Bisexual. Member, South Dakota State senate (2011–).

- **Micah Kellner** (1978–). Bisexual. Member, New York State Assembly (2007–2013).

- **JoCasta Zamarripa** (1976–). Bisexual. Member, Wisconsin State Assembly (2011–).

- **Waheed Alli** (1964–). Gay. Muslim. Member of the House of Lords, British Parliament.

- **J. Edgar Hoover** (1895–1972). Presumed gay. First director of the FBI (1935–1972).

- **Eleanor Roosevelt** (1882–1962). Presumed lesbian. First Lady of the United States (1933–1945).

- **Barbara Jordan** (1936–1996). Lesbian. Member of the US House of Representatives (1973–1979). Leader of the Civil Rights movement.

- **Deborah Batts** (1947–). Lesbian. First openly LGBT person to be appointed as federal judge (1994 by President Clinton).

- **Todd Hughes** (1960–). Gay. Fist openly LGBT judge to be appointed to US Circuit Court.

- **Georgina Beyer** (1957–). Transgender. World's first open transgender individual to be elected to Parliament (New

Zealand, 1999).

- **Michael Kirby** (1939–). Gay. Justice in Australia's High Court (1996–2009).

- **Edward II** (1284–1327). Bisexual. King of England.

- **Queen Christina** (1626–1689). Presumed lesbian. Queen of Sweeden (1632–1654).

- **Frederick the Great** (1712–1786). Presumed gay. King of Prussia (1772–1786).

- **Ferdinand I of Bulgaria** (1861–1948). Bisexual. Tsar of Bulgaria. Declared Bulgaria's independence from the Ottoman Empire.

RELIGION

- **Rev. Troy Perry** (1940–). Gay. Founder, Metropolitan Community Church.

- **Archbishop Carl Bean** (1944–). Gay. Founder, Unity Fellowship Church Movement. Made famous the song "I Was Born This Way" in 1977, well before Lady Gaga.

- **Bishop Gene Robinson** (1947–). Gay. Episcopalian Bishop of New Hampshire—first of any major Christian religion.

- **Bishop Mary Douglas Glasspool** (1954–). Lesbian. First open lesbian to become bishop in the Anglican faith.

- **Bishop Guy Erwin**. Gay. Bishop, Evangelical Lutheran Church in America.

- **Rabbi Sharon Kleinbaum** (1959–). Lesbian. Senior Rabbi of the largest LGBT synagogue in the world.

- **Rabbi Stephen Greenberg** (1956–). Gay. First openly gay Orthodox rabbi.

- **Imam Daayiee Adfullah** (1954–). Gay. American Muslim imam. Co-director, Muslims for Progressive Values. Board member, Al-Fatiha Foundation.

- **Irshad Manji** (1968–). Lesbian. Canadian Muslim author, journalist, and advocate. Director of Moral Courage Project and NY University. Books: *Allah, Liberty and Love*; *The Trouble with Islam Today*. Documentary: *Faith Without Fear*

- **John McNeill** (1925–). Gay. Theologian and former Jesuit. Author of multiple books, notably *The Church and the Homosexual* (1976).

- **Rev. Malcolm Boyd** (1923–). Gay. Priest, author of more than thirty books, and civil rights activist. Came out in 1977.

- **Mel White** (1940–). Gay. Clergyman and writer: *Stranger at the Gate; Lust: The Other Side of Love.*

MILITARY

- **Alexander the Great** (356–323 BC). Presumed gay. Emperor, who by age thirty had expanded his domain from Greece to Persia and to Egypt. One of the most successful military commanders of all time.

- **Hadrian** (76–138 AD). Presumed gay. Fourteenth Emperor of the Roman Empire.

- **T. E. Lawrence, "Lawrence of Arabia"** (1888–1935). Presumed gay. Liaison during the Arab Revolt. Writer: *Seven Pillars of Wisdom.*

- **Leonard Matlovich** (1943–1988). Gay. Vietnam War veteran, Purple Heart and Bronze Star. Tombstone reads: "A Gay Vietnam Veteran—When I was in the military, they gave me a medal for killing two men and a discharge for loving one."

- **Tammy S. Smith** (1963–). Lesbian. Brigadier General, US Army. First openly LGBT general in the United States military.

SCIENCE

- **Alan Turing** (1912–1954). Gay. Father of computer science and artificial intelligence. Mathematical genius who broke German codes during WWII. His breakthroughs shortened WWII and saved thousands of lives.

- **Baron John Maynard Keynes** (1883–1946). Bisexual. One of the most influential economists ever.

- **Lynn Conway** (1938–). Transgender. Creator of the methodology used to design all computer chips. Also invented method for high-performance computers.

- **Sally Ride** (1951–2012). Lesbian. Astronaut, physicist, engineer, and educator. First American woman in space. Youngest American to go into space (age 32).

- **Joan Roughgarden** (1946–). Transgender. Professor emeritus of biology, Stanford University. Author of eight scientific books.

- **Ben Barres**. Transgender. Chair, Neurobiology, Stanford University School of Medicine.

- **Deirdre McCloskey** (1942–). Transgender. Professor of economics, University of Illinois at Chicago. Author of numerous books.

- **Nate Silver** (1978–). Gay. Statistician, blogger, author. Accurately predicted the 2008 and 2012 US elections.

SPORTS

- **Caitlyn Jenner** (1949–). Transgender. Gold metal for decathlon ("World's Greatest Athlete"). TV personality.

- **Martina Navratilova** (1956–). Lesbian. Tennis player. All-time career record for men or women in singles and doubles.

- **Ian Thorpe** (1982–). Gay. Australian swimmer. Five Olympic gold medals.

- **Greg Louganis** (1960–). Gay. Four Olympic gold medals and five gold World Championships for diving. Best-selling author: *Breaking the Silence*.

- **Matthew Mitcham** (1988–). Gay. Australian Diver. Olympic gold medal.

- **Mildred "Babe" Zaharias** (1911–1956). Lesbian. One of the greatest athletes of the twentieth century. Two gold and one silver medals in 1932 Olympics. Multitalented: golf, basketball, track and field.

- **Sarah Vaillancourt** (1985–). Lesbian. Ice hockey player. Two Olympic gold metals.

- **Brian Boitano** (1963–). Gay. Olympic gold metal in figure skating.

- **Toller Cranston** (1949–). Gay. Figure skater. Canadian national champion. Bronze in 1976 Olympics.

- **Johnny Weir-Voronov** (1984–). Gay. American figure skater. Three time US national champion.

- **Gus Kenworthy** (1991–). Gay. Freestyle skier. Silver in 2014 Winter Olympics.

- **Renee Richards** (1934–). Transgender. Ophthalmologist, tennis player, and author.

- **Billie Jean King** (1943–). Lesbian. Professional tennis player.

- **Billy Bean** (1964–). Gay. Former Major League baseball player and author. Came out in 1999. Book: *Going the Other Way*.

- **Glenn Burke** (1952–1995). Gay. Former Major League baseball player. First and only Major League player known to be out to his team while a player.

- **Matthew Mitchman** (1988–). Gay. Olympic Gold for diving (2008) with the highest single-dive score in the history of the Olympics.

- **Tom Daley** (1994–). No Label. Olympic Bronze for diving (2012).

- **Ilana Kloss** (1956–). Lesbian. Tennis player. World Team Tennis commissioner.

- **David Kopay** (1942–). Gay. NFL player. One of the first athletes to come out (in 1975, after his retirement).

- **Roy Simmons** (1956–2014). Gay. NFL player. Came out in 1992 (after retirement).

- **Michael Sam** (1990–). Gay. First active NFL player to come out (2014).

- **Ian Roberts** (1965–). Gay. First rugby player to come out (1995).

- **Rosie Jones** (1959–). Lesbian. Golf player.

- **Orlando Cruz** (1981–). Gay. Professional boxer.

- **John Amaechi** (1974–). Gay. Basketball player.

- **Jason Collins** (1978–). Gay. Basketball player.

- **Robbie Rogers** (1987–). Gay. Soccer player.

- **Andrew Goldstein** (1983–). Gay. Lacrosse player.

BUSINESS

- **Sir Cecil Rhodes** (1853–1902). Presumed gay. Mining magnate. Founder of African state of Rhodesia. Funder of Rhodes scholarships.

- **Tim Cook** (1960–). Gay. CEO of Apple (2011–). One of the highest-paid executives ever ($376 million stock award in

2011).

- **Martine Rothblatt** (1954–). Transgender. Attorney, author, and entrepreneur. Founder and CEO, United Therapeutics.

- **John Browne** (1948–). Gay. CEO, British Petroleum (1995–2007). Member of House of Lords.

- **Rich Ross**. Gay. President of Discovery Channel (2015–).

- **Chris Hughes** (1983–). Gay. Cofounder, Facebook. Owner and publisher, *The New Republic*.

- **Jann Wenner** (1946–). Gay. Co-founder and publisher, *Rolling Stones*. Owner, *Men's Journal* and *US Weekly*.

- **Peter Thiel** (1967–). Gay. Entrepreneur, venture capitalist, and hedge fund manager. Early investor in Facebook.

- **Tim Gill** (1953–). Gay. Cofounder of software company Quark. Philanthropist and activist: Gill Foundation and Gill Action, which together invest about $20 million a year to promote equality for LGBT people.

- **David Bohnett** (1956–). Gay. Cofounder of GeoCities, sold to Yahoo in 1999. His foundation has given more than $45 million in grants.

- **Jon Stryker** (1958–). Gay. Billionaire heir to Stryker corporation. Philanthropist.

- **Jonathan Lewis** (1958–). Gay. Progressive Insurance. Investor and visionary philanthropist.

- **Linda Ketner** (1950–). Lesbian. Heir to Food Lion's business. Management consultant and philanthropist.

- **Bruce Bastian** (1948–). Gay. Cofounder, WordPerfect. Philanthropist.

- **Kathy Levinson** (1956–). Lesbian. Former chief operating officer and president, E*Trade. Three-sport varsity athlete.

Philanthropist.

- **Megan Smith** (1964–). Lesbian. Former Vice president, Google. Currently United States Chief Technology Officer.

- **Mitchell Gold**. Gay. Cofounder, Mitchell Gold+Bob Williams furniture. Cofounder, Faith In America. Philanthropist. Author.

- **Bob Page** (1945–). Gay. Founder, Replacements Limited. Philanthropist.

- **Charles Merrill, Jr.** (1920–). Bisexual. Author, artist, and philanthropist. Son of Merrill-Lynch founder.

- **R. Martin Chavez** (1964–). Gay. Chief Information officer and partner, Goldman Sachs.

- **Michael Bishop** (1942–). Gay. Businessperson. Majority owner of BMI airline, which he sold to Lufthansa. Net worth around $800 million.

- **Kevin McClatchy** (1963–). Gay. Businessperson. Principal owner, Pittsburgh Pirates (1996–2007).

LITERATURE AND THEATER

- **William Shakespeare** (1564–1616). Presumed bisexual. Poet and playwright. Considered greatest writer in the English language.

- **Tennessee Williams** (1911–1983). Gay. Writer and playwright: *A Streetcar Named Desire, Cat on a Hot Tin Roof*, and more.

- **André Gide** (1869–1951). Gay. Writer. Literature Nobel Prize, 1947.

- **Hans Christian Anderson** (1805–1875). Presumed gay. Most famous writer of fairy tales.

- **Walt Whitman** (1819–1892). Gay. Father of free verse. One of the greatest American poets.

- **Virginia Woolf** (1882–1941). Bisexual. Writer: *Mrs. Dalloway, To the Lighthouse, Orlando, A Room of One's Own*, and more.

- **Truman Capote** (1924–1984). Gay. Writer: *Breakfast at Tiffany's, In Cold Blood*, and more.

- **Gore Vidal** (1925–2012). Gay. Writer: *The City and the Pillar, The Best Man, The Last Empire*, and more.

- **Langston Hughes** (1902–1967). Presumed gay. Novelist, poet, playwright. Leader of Harlem Renaissance.

- **Ralph Waldo Emerson** (1803–1882). Bisexual. Writer. Leader of the Transcendentalist movement based on self-reliance.

- **E. M. Foster** (1879–1970). Gay. Novelist: *Where Angels Fear to Tread, The Longest Journey, A Room with a View, A Passage to India, Maurice*, and more.

- **Oscar Wilde** (1854–1900). Gay. Playwright and novelist: *The Importance of Being Earnest; Salome, The Picture of Dorian Gray,*

- **Thomas Mann** (1875–1955). Bisexual. Nobel Prize for Literature, 1929. Works: *Buddenbrooks, The Magic Mountain, Death in Venice*, and more.

- **James Baldwin** (1924–1987). Gay. Writer and civil rights activist. Books: *The Fire Next Time, Go Tell it on the Mountain*, and more.

- **Simone de Beauvoir** (1908–1986). Bisexual. Influential philosopher and writer. Companion of philosopher and author Jean-Paul Sartre.

- **Gertrude Stein** (1874–1946) and **Alice B. Toklas** (1877–1967). Lesbian couple. Writers, art collectors.

- **Dustin Lance Black** (1974–). Gay. Screenwriter. Oscar winner for *Milk* (Best Original Screenplay, 2008).

- **Sir Terence Rattigan** (1911–1977). Gay. Famous British playwright.

- **Harvey Fierstein** (1952–). Gay. Actor and playwright: *Torch Song Trilogy, La Cage aux Folles, A Catered Affair*.

- **Jean Cocteau** (1889–1963). Gay. French writer, artist, and filmmaker. Member: American Academy, French Academy, Royal Academy of Belgium, and German Academy.

- **Federico García Lorca** (1898–1936). Gay. Poet, dramatist, and theater director. One of the most important poets in the Spanish language.

- **Paul Verlaine** (1844–1896). Gay. Renowned French poet.

- **Arthur Rimbaud** (1854–1891). Gay. Prodigy French poet. Had long-term relationship with Paul Verlaine.

- **Armistead Maupin** (1944–). Gay. Writer: *Tales of the City* and more.

- **Alan Ball** (1955–). Gay. Writer, director, actor, producer. *American Beauty* (Oscar for Best Original Screenplay), *Six Feet Under*.

- **Andrew Tobias** (1947–). Gay. Writer about investments, coming out, other topics. Innovator in insurance. Treasurer, Democratic National Committee.

- **Adrienne Rich** (1929–2012). Lesbian. Poet, essayist, and feminist. Works: *A Change of World, Love Poems*, more.

- **Reinaldo Arenas** (1943–1990). Gay. Best-selling writer of *Before Night Falls, Farewell to the Sea*.

- **W. H. Auden** (1907–1973). Gay. Famous poet.

- **Rita Mae Brown** (1944–). Lesbian. Activist, novelist, poet, screenwriter. Well known for novel *Rubyfruit Jungle*.

- **Patricia Highsmith** (1921–1995). Lesbian. Writer. Film adaptations: *Strangers on a Train, Talented Mr. Rippley*...

- **Audre Lorde** (1934–1992). Lesbian. Writer, activist.

MUSIC

- **Pyotr Ilyich Tchaikovsky** (1840–1893). Gay. Russian composer of classical music.

- **Leonard Bernstein** (1918–1990). Gay. Renowned American composer and conductor.

- **Sir Elton John** (1947–). Gay. Singer, songwriter, and composer.

- **"Lady Gaga"—Stefani Joanne Angelina Germanotta** (1986–). Bisexual. Singer, songwriter, producer, actress.

- **"Boy George"—George Alan O'Dowd** (1961–). Gay. Singer and songwriter.

- **George Michael** (1963–). Gay. Musician, singer and songwriter.

- **Cole Porter** (1891–1964). Gay. Composer and songwriter. Married Linda Lee Thomas. His parties in Paris were renowned.

- **Joan Baez** (1941–). Bisexual. Folksinger and songwriter.

- **Ricky Martin** (1971–). Gay. Singer and actor.

- **Whitney Houston** (1963–2012). Presumed bisexual. Singer. Actress. The most-awarded female act of all time.

- **Sam Smith** (1992–). Gay. Singer and songwriter.

- **Aaron Copland** (1900–1990). Gay. Composer, conductor. Works include: *Third Symphony*.

- **Stephen Sondheim** (1930–). Gay. Award winning lyricist and composer: *Sweeney Todd, West Side Story,* others.

- **Earl Wild** (1915–2010). Gay. Virtuoso pianist.

- **Gladys Bentley** (1907–1960). Lesbian. Blues singer.

- **"Wendy and Lisa"– Wendy Melvoin** (1964–) **and Lisa Coleman** (1960–). Lesbian couple. Musicians in Prince's band and Emmy Award winning songwriters.

PAINTING, SCULPTURE

- **Leonardo da Vinci** (1452–1519). Presumed gay. Painter, sculptor, architect, scientist, musician, and inventor. One of the greatest geniuses of all time.

- **Michelangelo** (1475–1564). Presumed gay. One of the most famous painters, sculptors, architects, poets, and engineers of the Renaissance.

- **Andy Warhol** (1928–1987). Gay. Artist. Leader of the Pop Art movement.

- **David Hockney** (1937–). Gay. Pop art painter, print maker, and photographer.

FASHION

- **Cristobal Balenciaga** (1895–1972). Gay. Fashion designer. Founder of the Balenciaga *haute couture* house.

- **Gianni Versace** (1946–1997). Gay. Fashion designer. Founder of the Versace label.

- **Valentino Garavani** (1932–). Gay. Fashion designer. Founder of the Valentino brand and fashion house.

- **Tom Ford** (1961–). Gay. Fashion designer. Founder of the Ford label. Movie Director: *A Single Man.*

- **Charles Nolan** (1957–2011). Gay. Fashion designer. Founder of the Nolan label.

- **Marc Jacobs** (1963–). Gay. Designer. Founder of the Marc Jacobs label.

- **Bob Mackie** (1940–). Gay. Fashion designer.

- **"Lea T"—Leandra Madeiros Cerezo** (1981–). Transgender. Super model.

- **"Africa"—Tracey Norman** (1952–). Transgender. Super model.

- **Andreja Pejic** (1991–). Transgender. Super model.

MOVIES, ENTERTAINMENT, TV

- **Rock Hudson** (1925–1985). Gay. Actor who died of AIDS. His movies include: *Magnificent Obsession, Giant, Ice Station Zebra,* and *Dynasty.*

- **Sir Ian McKellen** (1939–). Gay. Actor.

- **George Takei** (1937–). Gay. Actor: *Star Trek.*

- **Angelina Jolie** (1975–). Bisexual. Actress, director, and humanitarian.

- **Ellen Degeneres** (1958–). Lesbian. Comedian, actress, TV show host.

- **Anderson Cooper** (1967–). Gay. Reporter, author, and TV anchor.

- **Rachel Maddow** (1973–). Lesbian. Author and TV host.

- **Don Lemon** (1966–). Gay. TV host.

- **Rosie O'Donnell** (1962–). Lesbian. TV show host, actress, comedian.

- **Andy Cohen** (1968–). Gay. TV host at Bravo.

- **Cynthia Nixon** (1966–). Bisexual. Actress.

- **Alvin Ailey, Jr.** (1931–1989). Gay. Founder, Alvin Ailey American Dance Theater in New York.

- **Josephine Baker** (1906–1975). Bisexual. Singer, dancer, actress, and activist. Significant contributions to the Civil Rights movement.

- **Rudolph Valentino** (1895–1926). Presumed gay. Famous actor in silent movies. Known as the Latin Lover. Married twice to women who presumably had lesbian relationships.

- **Marlon Brando** (1924–2004). Presumed bisexual. Actor. Named by the American Film Institute as the fourth greatest male American actor of all times. The book *Brando Unzipped* claims he had relationships with other famous actors, including James Dean, Cary Grant, John Gielgud, and Montgomery Clift.

- **Cary Grant** (1904–1986). Bisexual. Actor. The American Film Institute named him the Greatest Male Star of All Time. Movies: *The Philadelphia Story; To Catch a Thief; An Affair to Remember; North by Northwest*, among others.

- **Sir John Gielgud** (1904–2000). Gay. Actor, director, producer. One of few to win an Oscar, a Tony, an Emmy, and a Grammy.

- **Montgomery Clift** (1920–1966). Bisexual. Actor: *From Here to Eternity, A Place in the Sun, Confess,* and more. Nominated four times for Academy Awards.

- **Greta Garbo** (1905–1990). Bisexual. Actress: *Anna Christie, Grand Hotel.*

- **James Dean** (1931–1955). Gay. Iconic actor: *Rebel Without a Cause, East of Eden,* and *Giant.*

- **Anthony Perkins** (1932–1992). Gay. Oscar-winning actor. Died of AIDS.

- **Jodie Foster** (1962–). Lesbian. Actress, film director, and producer.

- **Sir Laurence Olivier** (1907–1989). Presumed bisexual. Renowned actor and director.

- **Tab Hunter** (1931–). Gay. Actor: *Battle Cry, That Kind of Woman.*

- **Ellen Page** (1987–). Lesbian. Actress: *Juno, Freeheld,* and more.

- **Laverne Cox**. Transgender. Actress, producer: *Orange is the New Black, Musical Chairs* and more.

- **Suze Orman** (1951–). Lesbian. Financial advisor, author, TV host.

- **David Geffen** (1943–). Gay. Film, theater, and music producer: *ET, Saving Private Ryan,* and more.

- **Chaz Bono** (1969–). Transgender. Writer and musician. Child of entertainers Sonny and Cher.

- **Ismail Merchant** (1936–2005) and **James Ivory** (1928–). Gay couple. Founders, Merchant Ivory productions. Films: *A Room with a View, Maurice, Mr. and Mrs. Bridge, Howards End.*

- **John Waters** (1946–). Gay. Film director, screenwriter, comedian. Films: *Hairspray, Cry Baby, Pecker,* and more.

- **Pier Paolo Pasolini** (1922–1975). Gay. Film director and writer. Films: *Teorema, Canterbury Tales,* and more.

- **Luchino Visconti** (1906–1976). Gay. Film, opera, and theater director. Films include *Death in Venice, The Leopard,* and *The Dammed.*

- **Pedro Almodóvar** (1949–). Gay. Oscar-winning Spanish filmmaker: *All About My Mother. Talk to Her.*

- **Lana Wachowski** (1965–). Transgender. Working as a team with brother Andy, they are filmmakers, screenwriters, and producers: The *Matrix* series of movies, and others.

- **James Randi** (1928–). Gay. Magician. Investigator of occult, paranormal, and supernatural claims.

- **Stephen Fry** (1957–). Gay. Actor, writer, comedian, host, activist.

- **Alan Ball** (1957–). Gay. Writer. Director. Producer. Work: *American Beauty, Six-Feet Under, True Blood,* and others.

CIVIC ENGAGEMENT

- **Harry Hay** (1912–2002). Gay. Renowned LGBT rights activist. Cofounder: Mattachine Society, Radical Faeries.

- **John Burnside III** (1916–2008). Gay. Activist (partner of Harry Hay for 40 years). Inventor of the kaleidoscope.

- **Del Martin** (1921–2008) and **Phyllis Lyon** (1924–). Lesbian couple. Renowned feminists and gay-rights activists. Founders of Daughters of Bilitis.

- **Larry Kramer** (1935–). Gay. Playwright, author, activist. Academy Award nominee. Finalist, Pulitzer Prize.

- **Frank Kameny** (1925–2011). Gay. Astronomer. Pioneer gay activist. Created slogan *"Gay is Good."*

- **Bayard Rustin** (1912–1987). Gay. Civil rights leader. Main organizer of the 1983 March on Washington.

- **Jane Addams** (1860–1935). Lesbian. First American woman to win the Nobel Peace Prize (1931).

- **Mary Bonauto** (1962–). Lesbian. Super Ace attorney for LGBT marriage and equal rights. MacArthur Fellow (2014).

- **Anthony Romero** (1965–). Gay. Executive Director ACLU since September 2001.

- **Thomas Stoddard** (1949–1997). Gay. Attorney. Former Executive of Lambda Legal. Activist for LGBT rights.

- **Roberta Achtenberg** (1950–). Lesbian. First openly LGBT person whose appointment required US Senate confirmation (1993, asst. secretary of Housing and Urban Development). Currently, commissioner, US Commission on Civil Rights.

- **Chai Feldblum** (1959–). Lesbian. Professor of law, Georgetown University. Chair, Equal Employment Opportunity Commission.

- **Axel and Eigil Axgil** (Axel: 1915–2011; Eigil: 1922–1995). Gay. First gay couple in the world to be joined in a registered domestic partnership (Denmark, 1989).

- **Ann Bancroft** (1955–). Lesbian. Adventurer, teacher, author. First woman to reach the North Pole by foot and sled. First woman to cross both the North and South Poles. First woman to ski across Greenland.

- **Katharine Lee Bates** (1859–1229). Presumed lesbian. Songwriter. Author of lyrics for *America the Beautiful*.

- **Baron Baden Powell** (1857–1941). Presumed gay. Army officer and writer. Considered the founder of the International Scouting Movement (Boy Scouts).

- **Laurence Michael Dillon** (1915–1962). Transgender. Physician, aristocrat, and first female-to-male transgender individual to undergo phalloplasty. Author: *Self—A Study in Endocrinology and Ethics*.

- **Kristin Beck** (1966–). Transgender. Former Navy Seal. Author: *Warrior Princess*.

- **Barbara Gittings** (1932–2007). Lesbian. Activist.

In addition, there are many other people who are committed to achieving equality for lesbian, gay, bisexual and transgender people. Here are just a few of them:

FOUNDERS OF NEW ORGANIZATIONS FOR EQUALITY (last 15 years)

- **Juan and Ken Ahonen-Jover** (eQualityGiving)

- **Tico Almeida** (Freedom to Work)

- **Wayne Besen** (Truth Wins Out)

- **Dana Beyer and Sharon Brackett** (Gender Rights Maryland)

- **David Brock** (EqualityMatters)

- **Linda Bush** (Movement Advancement Project)

- **Mitchell Gold and Jimmy Creech** (Faith in America)

- **Chad Griffin** (American Foundation for Equal Rights)

- **Georg Ketelhohn and Heddy Pena + 12 more** (Florida Together)

- **Carolyn Laub** (Gay Straight Alliance Network)

- **Robyn McGeehe and Kip Williams** (GetEqual)

- **Matt McTighe** (Freedom for All Americans)

- **Dan Savage** (It Gets Better)

- **Josh Seefried and Ty Walrod** (OutServe, which merged with SLDN)

- **Chuck Williams** (The Williams Institute)

- **Shane Windmeyer, Chad Wilson,** and **Sarah Holmes** (Campus Pride)

- **Evan Wolfson** (Freedom to Marry)

HEADS OF MAJOR NATIONAL ORGANIZATIONS FOR EQUALITY

- **Michael Adams** (Services and Advocacy for LGBT Elders, SAGE)

- **Gregory T. Angelo** (Log Cabin Republicans, LCR)

- **Aaron Belkin** (Palm Center)

- **Gabriel Blau** until October 2015 (Family Equality Council)

- **Eliza Byard** (Gay Lesbian & Straight Education Network, GLSEN)

- **Rea Carey** (The Task Force)

- **Heather Cronk** and **Angela Peoples** (GetEqual)

- **Jerame Davis** (Pride at Work)

- **Caroline Dessert** (Immigration Equality)

- **Sarah Kate Ellis** (GLAAD)

- **James Esseks** (ACLU LGBT Project)

- **Chad Griffin** (Human Rights Campaign, HRC)

- **Kris Hayashi** (Transgender Law Center)

- **Jody Huckaby** (Parents, Families and Friends of Lesbians and Gays, PFLAG)

- **Rebecca Isaacs** (Equality Federation)

- **Mara Keisling** (National Center for Transgender Equality, NCTE)

- **Kate Kendell** (National Center for Lesbian Rights, NCLR)

- **Abbe Land** (The Trevor Project)

- **Sharon Lettman-Hicks** (National Black Justice Coalition, NBJC)

- **Ricci Levy** (Woodhull Sexual Freedom Alliance)

- **Aisha Moodie-Mills** (Victory Fund)

- **Terry Stone** (CenterLink)

- **Matthew Thorne** (Outserve-SLDN)

- **Rachel B. Tiven** (Lambda Legal)

- **Janson Wu** (GLAD Gay & Lesbian Advocates & Defenders)

ORGANIZATIONS THAT HAVE ACHIEVED THEIR EQUALITY GOAL AND CLOSED THEIR DOORS

Thank you for a great job!

- **Freedom to Marry**

- **American Foundation for Equal Rights (AFER)**

- **Civil Marriage Collaborative**

CURRENT ACTIVISTS AND DONORS WHO ARE MAKING A DIFFERENCE

- **Henry van Ameringen,** strategic donor
- **Ron Ansin,** strategic donor
- **Chip Arndt,** activist and *Amazing Race* winner
- **John Bare,** activist donor
- **Jarrett Barrios,** strategist
- **Vic Basile,** strategist
- **Ignatius Bau,** strategist
- **Dana Beyer,** transgender activist and political candidate
- **Adam Bink,** grassroots activist
- **Marsha Botzer,** transgender activist
- **Jeff Campagna,** activist
- **Tom Carpenter,** strategist
- **Mandy Carter,** activist and Nobel Prize nominee

- **Jerry Chasen,** activist donor
- **Dan Choi,** DADT and equality activist
- **Bobby Clark,** online activist
- **Kate Clinton,** comedian
- **Michael Coe,** communicator
- **Matt Coles,** legal strategist
- **David da Silva Cornell,** activist
- **Anna Curren,** repeal DADT donor
- **Erin Drinkwater,** activist and doer
- **Stephen Driscoll,** democratic activist
- **Liebe and Seth Gadinsky,** allied donors
- **Brian Gaither,** activist
- **Chris Gates**, activist
- **Ethan Geto,** communications strategist
- **Don George,** activist donor
- **Lila Gracey,** strategist
- **Joe Falk,** political donor
- **J. Todd "Tif" Fernandez,** Equality Act activist
- **Matt Foreman,** strategist
- **Nathaniel Frank,** author
- **Stephen Handwerk,** Democratic activist
- **Craig Harwood,** donor and producer
- **Yashar Hedayat,** strategic donor
- **Stephen Herbits,** strategic doer, and donor
- **Joanne Herman,** transgender educator
- **Daniel Hernandez,** helping hand
- **Kelly Rivera Hart,** Latino and bi activist
- **Steve Hildebrand,** strategist
- **Donald Hitchcock,** strategist and activist
- **Ernest Hopkins,** activist
- **Bob Horvath,** political activist
- **Lane Hudson,** communications strategist and provocateur
- **Kathy James,** family advocate
- **Brian Johnson,** activist
- **Corey Johnson,** activist and councilman
- **Hans Johnson,** activist
- **Michael Kenny,** strategist and connector
- **Norm Kent,** publisher
- **Jon Kislak,** allied donor
- **Geoff Kors,** strategist
- **Lisa Kove,** Department of Defense activist
- **Michael Krawitz,** strategic donor
- **Janice Langbehn,** activist and 2011 US presidential Citizens medal recipient

- **Andrew Lane,** foundation executive director
- **Rodrigo Heng-Lehtinen,** trans activist
- **Jeff Lewy,** activist donor
- **Kerry Lobel,** strategist
- **Bill Lyons,** donor advisor
- **Barbara McCullough-Jones,** activist
- **Stuart Milk,** international activist
- **Richard Milstein,** donor
- **Shannon Price Minter,** transgender legal ace
- **Ineke Mushovic,** strategist
- **Kathryn Natale and Janet McLeod,** strategic donors
- **Christopher Neff,** journalist and publisher
- **Richard Noble,** walking activist
- **Derek Newton,** allied campaign strategist
- **CJ Ortuno,** activist ally
- **Dixon Osburn,** strategist
- **Kathy Padilla,** transgender activist
- **Jim Pepper,** strategic donor
- **Catherine Pino** and **Ingrid Duran,** strategists
- **Libby Post,** communicator
- **Bruce Presley,** donor and producer
- **Lisa Polyak,** marriage activist
- **Gautam Raghavan,** strategist
- **Donna Red Wing,** activist leader
- **Cathy Renna,** communications expert
- **Alix Ritchie and Marty Davis,** agitators
- **Laura Ricketts**, strategic donor
- **Cindy Rizzo,** human sexuality activist
- **Charles Robbins,** youth advocate
- **Mike Rogers,** blogger and citizen reporter
- **Charlie Rounds** and **Mark Hiemenz,** maverick donors
- **Hilary Rosen,** strategist
- **Marty Rouse,** grassroots activist
- **Caitlin Ryan,** family advocate and researcher
- **Rebecca Salokar,** professor and strategist
- **Diego Sanchez,** transgender activist
- **Marsha Scott,** donor strategist
- **Eugene Sepulveda,** donor
- **Garry Shay,** Democratic activist
- **Ken Sherrill,** political scientist
- **Joel Silberman,** media strategist
- **Howard Simon,** allied defender
- **Maryann Simpson,** donor

- **Barbra "Babs" Casbar Siperstein,** political compromiser
- **Richard Socarides,** activist
- **Palm Spaulding,** blogger activist
- **Rick Stafford,** Democratic activist
- **Anne Stanback,** marriage activist
- **Mark Steinberg** and **Dennis Edwards,** donors
- **Jim Stork,** strategist and donor
- **Sean Strub,** HIV activist
- **Andrew Sullivan,** author
- **Andy Szekeres,** fundraiser
- **Maxim Thorne,** strategist
- **Lisa Turner,** strategist
- **Urvashi Vaid,** author and strategist
- **Leoni Walker,** donor
- **Jillian Weiss,** transgender activist
- **Bernard Whitman,** communications expert
- **Sara Whitman,** activist donor
- **Jon Winkleman,** political activist
- **Bob Witeck,** communications expert
- **Paul Yandura,** donor strategist and revolutionary
- **Rich Yurko,** activist

APPENDIX 2:

The Dallas Principles

Below is the full text of the Dallas Principles (available at www.TheDallasPrinciples.com).

It is composed of: preamble, principles, full civil rights goals, and a call to action. The list of authors follows.

PREAMBLE

President Obama and Congress pledged to lead America in a new direction that included civil rights for lesbian, gay, bisexual and transgender Americans. We now sit at a great moment in our history that inspires the nation to return to its highest ideals and greatest promise. We face a historic opportunity to obtain our full civil rights; this is the moment for change. No delay. No excuses.

Nearly forty years ago, a diverse group of lesbian, gay, bisexual, and transgender people stood up to injustice at the Stonewall Inn in New York City. In doing so, they submitted themselves to bodily harm and criminal prosecution. Their demand was simple—equal protection under the law.

Still today, full civil rights has eluded the same community that rioted forty years ago. Instead, untold sums of resources have been spent to divide our nation and turn our lives into a political football.

At several junctures in American history, the stars have aligned to deliver the promise of equal protection under the law to those previously denied. At this unique time in history, our nation must once again exercise the great tradition of making its people equal.

Justice has too long been delayed. A clear path toward full civil equality for the LGBT community is overdue and must come now.

Using fear and misunderstanding to justify discrimination is no longer acceptable in this nation. Those content with the way things are will be judged harshly by history. Those who do not actively advance these ideals or offer excuses will be judged just as harshly. Those who attempt to divide our community or to delay and deny action on civil equality, waiting for the right moment to arrive, will be held accountable.

We reject the idea that honoring the founding principles of our country is controversial. We believe in the inherent human dignity of all people. No longer will we submit our children, our family, our friends, and ourselves as a political tool for any Party or ideology. A new day has arrived.

PRINCIPLES

The following eight guiding principles underlie our call to action. In order to achieve full civil rights now, we avow:

1. Full civil rights for lesbian, gay, bisexual and transgender individuals must be enacted now. Delay and excuses are no longer acceptable.

2. We will not leave any part of our community behind.

3. Separate is never equal.

4. Religious beliefs are not a basis upon which to affirm or deny civil rights.

5. The establishment and guardianship of full civil rights is a non-partisan issue.

6. Individual involvement and grassroots action are paramount to success and must be encouraged.

7. Success is measured by the civil rights we all achieve, not by words, access or money raised.

8. Those who seek our support are expected to commit to these principles.

FULL CIVIL RIGHTS GOALS

Being united by common principles and engaging in united action, we will achieve the following goals:

1. DIGNITY AND EQUALITY. Every lesbian, gay, bisexual, and transgender person has inherent dignity and worth, and has the right to live free of discrimination and harassment.

2. FAMILY. Every LGBT person has the right to a family without legal barriers to immigration, civil marriage, or raising children.

3. ECONOMIC OPPORTUNITY. Every LGBT person has the right to economic opportunity free from discrimination in employment, public housing, accommodation, public facilities, credit, and federally funded programs and activities.

4. EDUCATION. Every LGBT child and youth has the right to an education that is affirming, inclusive, and free from bullying.

5. NATIONAL SECURITY. Every LGBT person should have the opportunity to serve our

country openly and equally in our military and foreign service.

6. CRIME. Every LGBT person should enjoy life protected against bias crimes.

7. HEALTHCARE. Every person should have access to affordable, high quality, and culturally competent healthcare without discrimination.

CALL TO ACTION

1. We demand that government officials act now to achieve full civil rights without delay.

2. Our organizations and individuals need to develop a collaborative and revolutionary new organizing model that mobilizes millions of supporters through emerging web and phone technologies.

3. All LGBT individuals must accept personal responsibility to do everything within their power for equality and should get involved in the movement by volunteering, giving and being out.

4. We will hold elected officials and our organizations accountable for being transparent and achieving full civil rights by active participation when possible and active opposition when necessary.

5. Our allies need to be proactive in public support for full civil rights.

6. Every government measure that quantifies the US citizenry must permit LGBT individuals to self-identify and be counted in every way citizens are counted.

7. We demand that the media present LGBT lives in fair, accurate, and objective ways that neither include nor give credence to unsubstantiated, discriminatory claims and opinions.

AUTHORS

Here are the authors of the Dallas Principles with their affiliations at the time the principles were written.

- **Juan Ahonen-Jover, Ph.D.,** cofounder of eQualityGiving

- **Ken Ahonen-Jover, M.D.,** cofounder of eQualityGiving

- **John Bare,** activist donor

- **Senator Jarrett Barrios,** former Massachusetts legislator

- **Dana Beyer, M.D.,** transgender and political activist

- **Jeff Campagna, Esq.,** attorney and LGBT fundraiser and organizer

- **Mandy Carter,** Nobel Peace Prize nominee and lesbian activist

- **Michael Coe,** one of the "Most Influential Washingtonians under the Age of 40" according to *Washington Life Magazine*

- **Rev. Jimmy Creech,** straight ally working to end religion-based bigotry

- **Allison Duncan,** donor advisor

- **Ambassador Michael Guest,** senior advisor to the Council for Global Equality

- **Joanne Herman,** donor and transgender rights advocate

- **Donald Hitchcock,** activist and former executive director, Gay and Lesbian Leadership Council

- **Lane Hudson,** political activist and one of the "Most Influential Gay People in America" according to *Out Magazine*

- **Charles Merrill,** philanthropist (Merrill-Lynch family), activist, and artist

- **Dixon Osburn, Esq.,** cofounder, former executive director, Servicemembers Legal Defense Network

- **Lisa Polyak,** lead plaintiff in litigation to obtain marriage equality in Maryland

- **Babs Casbar Siperstein,** transgender activist and board member

- **Pam Spaulding,** editor and publisher, www.PamsHouseBlend.com

- **Andy Szekeres,** political consultant and fundraiser

- **Lisa Turner,** political consultant and donor advisor

- **Jon Winkleman,** political activist

- **Paul Yandura,** political strategist and donor advisor

APPENDIX 3:

Good Companies

Listed below by industry are the companies with a 100-percent rating in the 2016 Corporate Equality Index compiled by the Human Rights Campaign (www.hrc.org/cei). Note that this list is not exhaustive since there might be companies with a 100-percent rating that have not reported to the Human Rights Campaign.

ADVERTISING AND MARKETING
- Digitas
- Interpublic Group of Companies
- Leo Burnett Company
- MSLGROUP Americas
- Ogilvy Group
- Publicis Healthcare Communications
- Publicis
- Razorfish
- Re:Sources USA (new)
- Saatchi & Saatchi North America (new)
- Starcom MediaVest Group
- ZenithOptimedia

AEROSPACE AND DEFENSE
- Boeing
- Harris (new)
- Lockheed Martin
- Northrop Grumman
- Raytheon
- Rockwell Collins (new)

AIRLINES
- Alaska Air Group
- American Airlines
- Jet Blue
- Southwest (new)
- United Airlines

APPAREL, FASHION, TEXTILES, DEPARTMENT STORES
- Adidas North America (new)
- American Apparel (new)
- Levi Strauss & Co.
- Macy's
- Nike

AUTOMOTIVE
- Ford
- General Motors
- Nissan North America
- Tesla
- Toyota
- Wolkswagen Group of America

BANKING AND FINANCIAL SERVICES
- AllianceBernstein (new)
- American Express
- Ameriprise Financial
- Bank of America
- Bank of New York Mellon
- Barclays
- BlacRock
- BNP Paribas
- Capital Markets
- Capital One
- Charles Schwab
- Citigroup
- Comerica
- Credit Suisse USA
- Depository Trust & Clearing Corp.
- Deutsche Bank
- Discover Financial Services
- Eastern Bank
- Fannie Mae
- Federal Reserve Bank of Atlanta
- Federal Reserve Bank of Boston
- Federal Reserve Bank of Cleveland (new)
- First Data
- Freddie Mac
- Goldman Sachs
- Huntington Bancshares
- JP Morgan Chase

- KeyCorp
- MasterCard
- Moody's
- Morgan Stanley
- Northern Trust
- PNC Financial Services Group
- Prudential Financial
- RBC Capital Markets
- RBC Wealth Management
- Rockland Trust (new)
- State Street
- SunTrust Banks
- Synchrony Financial (new)
- T. Rowe Price
- TD Ameritrade (new)
- TD Bank
- TD Securities (new)
- Teachers Insurance & Annuity Association
- US Bancorp
- UBS AG
- Union Bank
- Vanguard Group (new)
- Visa
- Wells Fargo

CHEMICALS AND BIOTECHNOLOGY
- BASF
- Dow Chemical
- Ecolab
- Genentech
- Monsanto
- Thermo Fisher Scientific

COMPUTER AND DATA SERVICES
- Automatic Data Processing
- Broadridge Financial Solutions
- Dell (new)
- Dropbox (new)
- EMC
- FactSet Research Systems (new)
- Hewlett-Packard
- Tech Data

COMPUTER HARDWARE AND OFFICE EQUIPMENT
- Apple
- Lexmark International
- NCR
- Xerox

COMPUTER SOFTWARE
- Adobe Systems
- CA Technologies
- Electronic Arts
- Intuit
- Microsoft
- Oracle
- SAP America
- Symantec
- Uber Technologies (new)

CONSULTING AND BUSINESS SERVICES
- A.T. Kearney
- Accenture
- Aon
- Bain & Co./Bridgespan Group
- Booz Allen Hamilton
- Boston Consulting Group
- CEB (new)
- Convergys (new)
- Deloitte
- Ernst & Young
- Huron Consulting Group
- IBM
- KPMG
- Manpower Group (new)
- Marsh & McLennan Companies
- McKinsey & Co.
- Navigant Consulting
- Nielsen
- PricewaterhouseCoopers
- Slalom Consulting
- Thomson Reuters
- Towers Watson

EDUCATION AND CHILD CARE
- Pearson

ENERGY AND UTILITIES
- Exelon
- PG&E
- Portland General Electric
- Sempra Energy
- Southern California Edison

ENGINEERING AND CONSTRUCTION
- Turner Construction (new)

ENTERTAINMENT AND ELECTRONIC MEDIA
- AMC Entertainment
- CBS
- Comcast
- Direct TV
- Sirius XM Radio
- Sony Corporation of America (new)
- Sony Pictures Entertainment
- Time Warner
- Viacom
- Walt Disney

FOOD, BEVERAGES AND GROCERIES
- Anheuser-Busch
- Aramak
- Barilla America
- Ben & Jerry's (new)
- Brown-Forman
- Campbell Soup
- Cargill
- Coca-Cola
- ConAgra Foods
- Darden Restaurants
- Delhaize America
- Diageo North America
- E&J Gallo Winery
- General Mills
- Hershey
- Hormel Foods (new)
- Kellogg
- Kraft Foods
- Land O'Lakes
- McDonald's (new)
- MillerCoors

- Mondelez International
- PepsiCo
- Sodexo
- WhiteWave Foods (new)

FOREST AND PAPER PRODUCTS
No companies in this industry reporting 100 percent rating

HEALTHCARE / HEALTH INSURANCE
- Aetna
- Blue Cross Blue Shield of North Carolina
- Boston Scientific (new)
- Cardinal Health
- CareFusion
- Cigna (new)
- CVS Health
- Henri Schein (new)
- Exellus Health Plan
- Humana
- Kaiser Permanente
- McKesson

HEALTHCARE / MEDICAL FACILITIES
No companies in this industry reporting 100 percent rating

HIGH-TECH / PHOTO / SCIENCE EQUIPMENT
- Eastman Kodak
- HERE North America
- Intel
- Medtronic
- NVIDIA (new)

HOME FURNISHING
- IKEA (new)
- Mitchell Gold + Bob Williams

HOTELS, RESORTS AND CASINOS
- Borgata Hotel Casino & Spa (new)
- Caesars Entertainment
- Choice Hotels International
- Hilton Worldwide
- Hyatt Hotels
- InterContinental Hotels
- Kimpton Hotel & Restaurant Group

- Marriott International
- MGM Resorts
- Starwood Hotels & Resorts
- The Cosmopolitan of Las Vegas
- Wynn Resorts

INSURANCE
- AIG
- American Family Insurance Group (new)
- Anthem (new)
- AXA Equitable Life Insurance
- Blue Cross and Blue Shield of Rhode Island
- Blue Cross and Blue Shield of Florida
- Blue Cross and Blue Shield of Massachusetts (new)
- Chubb
- CNA Insurance (new)
- CSAA Insurance
- Erie Insurance Group (new)
- Excellus Health Plan (new)
- Genworth Financial (new)
- Hartford Financial Services
- Harvard Pilgrim Health Care
- John Hancock Financial Services
- Lincoln National (new)
- Massachusetts Mutual Life Insurance
- MedLife
- Nationwide
- New York Life Insurance
- Northwestern Mutual Life Insurance
- Principal Financial Group (new)
- State Farm (new)
- Sun Life Financial
- Travelers (new)
- Voya Financial

INTERNET SERVICES AND RETAILING
- Airbnb (new)
- eBay
- Facebook
- Google
- Groupon
- Paypal (new)
- Twitter (new)
- WeddingWire (new)

- Yahoo!
- Yelp

LAW FIRMS
Ninety-five law firms report a 100 percent rating (six more than in 2015)

MAIL AND FREIGHT DELIVERY
No companies in this industry reporting 100 percent rating

MANUFACTURING
- 3M
- Ball (new)
- Corning
- Cummins
- Danaher
- Eaton (new)
- General Electric
- Herman Miller
- Nestle Purina Pet Care (new)
- Owens Corning
- Rockwell Automation
- Steelcase

MINING AND METALS
- Alcoa

MISCELLANEOUS
- E.I. du Pont (new)
- W.W. Grainger

OIL AND GAS
- Chevron
- Shell (new)

PHARMACEUTICALS
- AbbVie (new)
- Astellas Pharma
- Baxter (new)
- Biogen
- Boehringer Ingelheim USA
- Bristol-Myers Squibb
- Eli Lilly
- Johnson & Johnson

- Merck
- Novartis Pharmaceuticals
- Pfizer

PUBLISHING AND PRINTING
No companies in this industry reporting 100 percent rating

REAL ESTATE, COMMERCIAL
- CBRE
- JLL

REAL ESTATE, RESIDENTIAL
No companies in this industry reporting 100 percent rating

RETAIL AND CONSUMER PRODUCTS
- Abercrombie & Fitch
- American Eagle Outfitters
- Avon
- Barnes & Noble
- Best Buy
- Caleres (new)
- Clorox
- Coach
- Estee Lauder (new)
- GameStop
- Gap
- Hallmark Cards (new)
- Home Depot (new)
- J.C. Penney (new)
- Mattel (new)
- Newell Rubbermaid
- Nordstrom
- Office Depot
- Outerwall (new)
- Procter & Gamble
- Replacements
- S.C. Johnson & Son (new)
- Sears
- Sony Electronics
- Staples
- Starbucks
- Target
- TJX
- Uniliver

- Walgreens
- Whirpool (new)

TELECOMMUNICATIONS
- Alcatel-Lucent
- AT&T
- Cisco
- Level 3 Communications (new)
- QUALCOMM
- Sprint
- Time Warner Cable
- T-Mobile USA

TOBACCO
No companies in this industry reporting 100 percent rating

TRANSPORTATION AND TRAVEL
- American Express Global Business Travel (new)
- Orbitz Worldwide
- Royal Caribbean (new)

WASTE MANAGEMENT
No companies in this industry reporting 100 percent rating

APPENDIX 4:

Equality Act

This act was introduced in Congress on July 23, 2015 by Representative David Cicilline (D-RI) and Senator Jeff Merkley (D-OR) and has 172 cosponsors in the House and 40 in the Senate as of February 5, 2016.

Below is the bill summary. The full text of the Equality Act is available on Congress' website:
www.congress.gov/bill/114th-congress/house-bill/3185

BILL SUMMARY

Amends the Civil Rights Act of 1964 to include sex, sexual orientation, and gender identity among the prohibited categories of discrimination or segregation in places of public accommodation.

Defines:
- "sex" to include a sex stereotype, sexual orientation or gender identity, and pregnancy, childbirth, or a related medical condition;
- "sexual orientation" as homosexuality, heterosexuality, or bisexuality; and
- "gender identity" as gender-related identity, appearance, mannerisms, or characteristics, regardless of the individual's designated sex at birth.

Expands the categories of public accommodations to include places or establishments that provide:
- exhibitions, recreation, exercise, amusement, gatherings, or displays;
- goods, services, or programs, including a store, a shopping center, an online retailer or service provider, a salon, a bank, a gas station, a food bank, a service or care center, a shelter, a travel agency, a funeral parlor, or a health care, accounting, or legal service; or

- transportation services.

Prohibits "establishment" from being construed to be limited to a physical facility or place.

Authorizes the Department of Justice (DOJ) to bring a civil action if it receives a complaint from an individual who claims to be:
- denied equal utilization of a public facility owned, operated, or managed by a state (other than public schools or colleges) on account of sex, sexual orientation, or gender identity; or
- denied admission to, or not permitted to continue attending, a public college by reason of sexual orientation or gender identity, thereby expanding DOJ's existing authority to bring such actions for complaints based on race, color, religion, sex, or national origin.

Revises public school desegregation standards to provide for the assignment of students without regard to sexual orientation or gender identity.

Prohibits programs or activities receiving federal financial assistance from denying benefits to, or discriminating against, persons based on sex, sexual orientation, or gender identity.

Prohibits employers with 15 or more employees from discriminating based on sexual orientation or gender identity, subject to the same exceptions and conditions that currently apply to unlawful employment practices based on race, color, religion, sex, or national origin.

Requires employers to recognize individuals in accordance with their gender identity if sex is a bona fide occupational qualification that is reasonably necessary to the normal operation of that particular business or enterprise.

Provides government employees with protections against discrimination based on sexual orientation or gender identity.

Authorizes DOJ to intervene in equal protection actions in federal court on account of sexual orientation or gender identity.

Requires protections against discrimination based on race, color, religion, sex, sexual orientation, gender identity, or national origin to include protections against discrimination based on: (1) an association with another person who is a member of such a protected class; or (2) a perception or belief, even if inaccurate, that an individual is a member of such a protected class. Prohibits the Religious Freedom Restoration Act of 1993 from providing a claim, defense, or basis for challenging such protections.

Prohibits an individual from being denied access to a shared facility, including a restroom, a locker room, and a dressing room, that is in accordance with the individual's gender identity.

Amends the Fair Housing Act, the Equal Credit Opportunity Act, and jury selection standards to add sexual orientation and gender identity as classes protected against discrimination under such laws.

APPENDIX 5:

What We Accomplished 2012-15

Each edition of the *Gay Agenda* starts with a summary of what we accomplished in the prior year. Below are the summaries for all editions of this book.

WHAT WE ACCOMPLISHED IN 2012

Here are the most significant advances for LGBT equality in 2012:

- President Obama came out in favor of the freedom to marry the person you love.

- LGBT voters voted 76 percent for Obama versus 22 percent for Romney. This disparity, with the support of other minority voters, gave Obama the victory in states like Florida and Ohio.

- The people of Maryland voted to allow same-gender couples to get married.

- The people of Washington State voted for the same right.

- So did the people in Maine, for a total of nine states plus the District of Columbia that supported same-gender marriage in 2012.

- The people of Minnesota voted down a constitutional amendment that would have enshrined discrimination in their state constitution by limiting marriage to different-gender couples. In an unprecedented win, the four ballot initiatives regarding marriage were won by the supporters of equality.

- The people of Wisconsin elected Tammy Baldwin to the US Senate, the first openly LGBT person in that position.

- The people of Colorado, Rhode Island, Arizona, New York, California, and Wisconsin elected openly LGB people to represent them in the US House of Representatives. With a total of six LGB representatives, this is an all-time record. For the first time, an openly bisexual person, Kyrsten Sinema was elected to Congress representing Arizona—alas, no transgender member of Congress yet.

- For the first time in seven state legislatures, the people elected an openly LGBT person to represent them. In addition, the Washington senate elected Ed Murray (who is openly gay) as its majority leader. Moreover, the Colorado House of Representatives elected Mark Ferrandino (who is openly gay) as its speaker, and Oregon's House voted Tine Kotek (who is openly lesbian) as its speaker. They joined Gordon Fox, who has been the openly gay speaker of Rhode Island's House of Representatives since 2010.

- The Equal Employment Opportunity Commission ruled unanimously that transgender people are protected against employment discrimination under Title VII of the Civil Rights Act. Several other court rulings and agency rulings advanced employment nondiscrimination for transgender people, including protection under the Fourteenth Amendment to the US Constitution.

- Finally, in December 2012, the American Psychiatric Association removed gender identity disorder as a mental disease.

These unprecedented victories provide great momentum for a full-out action to finally achieve LGBT equality now.

WHAT WE ACCOMPLISHED IN 2013

Two important decisions of the Supreme Court in June 2013 paved the way for significant advances in legal equality for lesbian, gay, bisexual, and transgender (LGBT) Americans. Here are the main advances in 2013:

- The Supreme Court ruled that the plaintiffs appealing the California marriage case did not have standing, in effect allowing same-gender marriages to resume for good in the largest state. This meant that an additional 12% of the US population was granted the right to marry the person they love.

- In a second decision, the Supreme Court also required the federal government to recognize all legal marriages performed by a state. As a result, the Obama administration took swift action giving all 1,138 rights and obligations of marriage to all couples who lived in a state where same-gender marriage is legal. For couples in other states, the administration gave as many rights as allowed by then current federal law, including sponsoring the spouse for immigration, benefits to service members, and the right to file federal taxes as a married couple. However, social security benefits were still not available to same-gender couples who lived in a discriminatory state, although the administration is studying whether there are alternatives.

- A record of eight states added the freedom to marry in 2013, in addition to Utah which was under appeal. From a total of nine states and the District of Columbia in 2012 to seventeen states and DC in 2013. Once the new law took effect in Illinois (in June 2014), thirty-eight percent of the American population was living in a state with marriage equality. Five states added the freedom to marry through their legislatures: Rhode Island, Delaware, Minnesota, Illinois, and Hawai'i. Three states added it through the courts: California, New Jersey, and New Mexico. In addition, a federal district court allowed same-gender couples to marry in Utah; this decision was now under appeal in 2013.

- The Employment NonDiscrimination Act (ENDA) passed the US Senate in November 2013, but the Republican speaker of the House did not bring it up for a vote, although expectations were that if House members were allowed to vote their conscience instead of the party line, it would have a majority.

- In November 2013, Congressman Michael Michaud (D-ME) came out as gay. He became the seventh member of the US House of Representatives who is openly gay or bisexual (but none is lesbian or transgender). There is only one member of the US Senate who is openly LGBT, Tammy Baldwin (D-WI).

- As of 2012, there were only two states (Connecticut and Vermont) who offered total legal equality for its LGBT citizens. In 2013 California and the District of Columbia were added to the list of states offering full equality. This brought it to 16 percent of the American population living in a state with full legal equality for its LGBT citizens.

- Colorado upgraded its domestic reciprocal beneficiaries act to civil unions and Oregon started recognizing same-gender marriages performed in other states and foreign countries (in both states, marriage equality was forbidden by a state constitutional amendment).

- In Delaware, the Democratic governor signed into law marriage equality and legislation to add gender identity to its non discrimination and hate crimes statutes.

- In Nevada, the Republican governor signed into law legislation that added gender identity to its hate crimes statute.

- The Washington DC council unanimously passed the JaParker Deoni Jones Birth Certificate Amendment Act, considered by many as the model bill in the United States for equal treatment of transgender people regarding their birth certificates.

- President Obama appointed five gay men as ambassadors: John Berry to Australia, Rufus Gifford to Denmark, James Costos to Spain, James "Wally" Brewster to the Dominican Republic, and Daniel Baer to the Organization for Security and Cooperation in Europe. He also appointed Todd Hughes to the US Court of Appeals, the first gay man appointed to such position.

- After four decades, Exodus International accepted that sexual orientation cannot be changed and shut down its operations. This organization had worked to change sexual orientation through prayer and so-called reparative therapies.

WHAT WE ACCOMPLISHED IN 2014

The expansion of equal rights after the two 2013 Supreme Court decisions continued at an unprecedented pace.

Here are the main advances in 2014:

- At the end of 2013, same-gender couples could marry in seventeen states (and the District of Columbia). One year later, the number was thirty-five with two more states added early in 2015. This means that more than seventy percent of the population was covered by the right to marry the person they love (from thirty-eight percent) a year earlier.

- Oregon and Washington state now provide full equality to their LGBT residents. They joined California, Connecticut, Vermont, and the District of Columbia in reaching equality.

- President Obama signed an expansion of two prior executive orders protecting federal employees and employees of federal contractors from discrimination due to sexual orientation and gender identity.

- The Obama administration continued making available to same-gender couples the same federal benefits that are available to other married couples. This was not possible in all cases, since some federal benefits were only available, by the law at the time, to couples living in a state that recognized their marriage. Among the protections expanded is making the benefits of the Family and Medical Leave Act available to all couples.

- Article 125 of the Military Code of Justice was repealed. It forbid certain sexual practices between consenting adults of either gender.

- Defeated several antigay bills that could discriminate LBGT people under the banner of religious liberty, in states such as Arizona, Georgia, Hawaii, Idaho, Kansas, Maine, Mississippi, Missouri, Ohio, Oklahoma, South Dakota, and Tennessee.

- In June, the Presbyterian Church allowed same-gender marriage, joining the United Church of Christ, Quakers, Reform and Conservative Judaism, among others.

- All six openly LGBT members of the United States House of Representatives were re-elected in the November election.

- Also in November, Massachusetts elected its first openly gay Attorney General.

- Ted Osius was confirmed by the Senate to serve in Vietnam as ambassador. There are seven openly gay ambassadors appointed by President Obama (but none openly lesbian, bisexual or transgender).

- At the end of the year, the Justice Department agreed that transgender individuals who are discriminated are protected by Title VII of the Civil Rights Act of 1964.

WHAT WE ACCOMPLISHED IN 2015

Here are the main advances in 2015:

- The US Supreme Court ruled that the US Constitution requires that all states and territories make the fundamental right of marriage available to all couples, independently of their sexual orientation. *This is the biggest victory for LGBT equality ever.*

  Gallup estimated that by the end of 2015 there were about one million Americans in same-sex marriages.

- The Equal Employment Opportunity Commission (EEOC) ruled that discrimination in employment due to sexual orientation is a form of sex discrimination. In 2012, the EEOC had a similar ruling regarding gender identity. By the charter of this commission, these rulings only apply to employment and not to housing, public accommodations, or credit.

- In several states, succeeded in stopping "freedom of religion" legislation that was intended to deny services and discriminate against LGBT people, as well as several "bathroom" laws that required transgender people to use the bathroom matching their gender at birth. Unfortunately, we did not win all these battles yet.

- The congressional LGBT Equality Caucus created a Task Force on Transgender Equality addressing the legislative needs for the community including health care, violence, unemployment, and homelessness. It is composed of eight members of congress (including Ileana Ros-Lehtinen (R-FL) who has a transgender son and Mike Honda (D-CA) who has a transgender granddaughter).

- Salt Lake City elected Jackie Biskupski, an openly lesbian, as its mayor.

- Pennsylvania confirmed Dr. Rachel Levine, a transgender woman, as its Physician General.

- The Boys Scouts of America rescinded the ban on gay adults being leaders of the organization. In 2013 the organization had removed the ban on gay youth being a member.

- Several courts ruled in favor on multiple cases challenging LBGT equality.

www.ingramcontent.com/pod-product-compliance
Lightning Source LLC
Chambersburg PA
CBHW071331280526
45787CB00001B/65